FISH

DELICIOUS RECIPES FOR FISH & SHELLFISH

MASTERCHEF WINNER 2009

MAT FOLLAS

PHOTOGRAPHY BY STEVE PAINTER

RYLAND PETERS & SMALL
LONDON • NEW YORK

PHOTOGRAPHY, DESIGN, AND PROP STYLING Steve Painter
COMMISSIONING EDITOR Stephanie Milner
PRODUCTION CONTROLLER David Hearn
ART DIRECTOR Leslie Harrington
EDITORIAL DIRECTOR Julia Charles
PUBLISHER Cindy Richards

FOOD STYLIST Lucy McKelvie
INDEXER Hilary Bird

First published in 2015 by
Ryland Peters & Small
20–21 Jockey's Fields
London WC1R 4BW
and
341 E 116th St
New York NY 10029

www.rylandpeters.com

10 9 8 7 6 5 4 3 2 1

Text © Mat Follas 2015
Design and photographs © Ryland Peters & Small 2015
All photography by Steve Painter excluding page 33
by Jan Baldwin

Printed in China

ISBN: 978-1-84975-605-1

A CIP record for this book is available from the British Library.

US Library of Congress CIP data has been applied for.

NOTES
• Both British (Metric) and American (Imperial plus US cups)
are included in these recipes for your convenience, however
it is important to work with one set of measurements and
not alternate between the two within a recipe.
• All spoon measurements are level unless otherwise specified.
• All eggs are medium (UK) or large (US), unless specified as
large, in which case US extra-large should be used. Uncooked
or partially cooked eggs should not be served to the very old,
frail, young children, pregnant women or those with
compromised immune systems.
• Ovens should be preheated to the specified temperatures.
We recommend using an oven thermometer. If using a
fan-assisted oven, adjust temperatures according to the
manufacturer's instructions.
• Whenever butter is called for within these recipes, unsalted
butter should be used.
• When a recipe calls for the grated zest of citrus fruit, buy
unwaxed fruit and wash well before using. If you can only find
treated fruit, scrub well in warm soapy water before using.

CONTENTS

INTRODUCTION

I have lived the wild life for as long as I can remember. An absent naval father and a stepmother who made no secret of her dislike for parenting duties meant my formative years in New Zealand were spent running wild. My brother and I would swim in a nearby river, jumping off a road bridge into it, we'd play chicken with trains on a nearby train track and generally do all the things young boys without a lot of parental guidance were likely to do. We were lucky, we never got seriously hurt or in too much trouble and I was shunted off to boarding school at age 10 when my parents left the country to move to the USA.

I remember following eel trails across the grass on dewy mornings, as the eels were seeking new water, the unlucky ones would be caught and, in a scene reminiscent of *The Lord of the Flies*, would lose their heads, skin and become a barbecue treat for us.

Slightly older, we moved to Auckland for a few years and lived close to the sea. My adventures became focused around the local wharf and beaches. I had an old inflated inner tube that I'd sit in and float around under my local wharf, dodging fishing lines from the fishermen gathered above. I'd hunt for fishing lures stuck on rocks to sell to the fishermen and would happily gorge on fresh mussels from the wharf piles as I explored. Walks on the beach nearby were to find pipis (native clams) and cockles, taken home to be cooked and eaten with some malt vinegar, a treat I still love today. I was inspired to create my Rockpool Soup with Squid, Clams, Mussels, Seaweed & Samphire on page 124 that offers a taste of the seashore by these early foraging adventures.

I learnt to fish and through cheek and word of mouth had a regular round of cat owners who would buy my sprats and other small fish from me for a few cents each, it was only after a while I realized what a treat they were to eat, although I'm sure they would be well under any minimum catch size nowadays. As delighted as I was to escape my stepmother's regime, when I was told I was going to boarding school I was also upset at the loss of income as I had to give up my beloved fish round.

Boarding school is a blur of rugby, cold swims, canteen food and some pretty fierce discipline but also some inspirational teachers and a moral code that will never leave me. I won't pretend I enjoyed it though.

At age 16 I was fending for myself, an apprenticeship at the local naval dockyards was my lifeline and my hobbies were motorbikes and anything that took me outdoors – they still are. I had a great interest in bush walking (called 'tramping' in New Zealand) and often spent several days alone in native bush land crossing some of the amazing peninsulas and national parks dotted within a few hours' bike ride from Auckland. I'd survive off dehydrated rations and anything I could find or catch along the way; seashore foraging for shellfish and crabs made for simple but delicious meals. As my income grew I took up scuba diving and my foraging yielded treats from the sea: fish, lobster and scallops. I'd add seaweeds and kina (sea urchin) to my catch pot and would have some truly amazing feasts. Try some of the wonderful crustacean and shellfish recipes in the penultimate chapter of the book. Eating food prepared fresh produces delicious flavours and satisfaction that I love to reproduce today, even if it is now usually someone else doing the hard work to catch it.

More than a few years on and my wife and I moved to Dorset in the UK, I took up diving again and many of the same ingredients from my youth have become my family's treats, too. Cooking, which had always been a hobby, became a passion as I now had a ready audience of family and friends and a free supply of wonderful seafood and produce all around me.

In 2008 I made a spur of the moment decision to apply for the TV series MasterChef with the dream of opening my own café or restaurant if it turned out I could cook to a decent standard. I managed to win the series and, off the back of the publicity that generated, opened my first restaurant The Wild Garlic in my local town. The Wild Garlic was a success gaining reviews of 9½/10 in the *Guardian* and 9/10 in the *Telegraph* newspapers and recommendations in *The Michelin Guide*, *The Good Food Guide* and *The AA Restaurant Guide*, which awarded it two rosettes for culinary excellence. Most of the recipes in this book take their inspiration from our menus at The Wild Garlic and my own cooking at home. They have been modified slightly to include only ingredients that should be readily available for you at home.

Some of the dishes I cooked on MasterChef have inspired recipes in this book, the Crab Thermidor on page 151, Scallop Chowder on page 133 and the beautiful Clams with Caper Mayonnaise on page 141 are all from dishes that I cooked on the show.

From The Wild Garlic are classic recipes which helped us win awards. My favourites include Dover Sole Meunière on page 93, Trout en Papillote on page 37, Teriyaki Salmon on page 16 and Halibut Steak with Cider Cream Sauce, Crackling & Mash on page 105, these dishes have been cooked hundreds of times and keep the customers returning time after time for more.

A summer restaurant we ran on Chesil Beach during the Olympic sailing in Dorset specialized in seafood and our Bouillabaisse was reviewed as 'easily the best Bouillabaisse I've ever tasted' by the *Telegraph* – try it for yourself, following the recipe on page 74.

Many people are scared of seafood because of bones or the complexity of filleting fish. I have included some guides for how to do this yourself but, in the same way you expect meat to be portioned by a butcher, you should ask your fishmonger to prepare the fish for you.

These recipes are tried and tested over years of kitchen use, the majority are quick and easy to prepare, I wholeheartedly recommend them to you to try and enjoy at home.

SUSTAINABILITY, CONSERVATION & CHOOSING FISH

This book is about celebrating the wonderful and diverse choices for cooking fish and seafood not debating fishery methods but it would be irresponsible not to discuss the sourcing of fish, too, especially as some of my recipes do use fish varieties that should be sourced with care. Many of the recipes featured here can be made using a selection of fish or shellfish, so try substituting similar styles and use the best quality fish you can source.

Fish, in my opinion, should be our main source of protein as it has the lowest environmental impact to produce of any animal proteins, only battery-bred chickens coming close, and I personally don't want to eat battery chickens.

Wild fish, although having a low environmental impact, are generally expensive and have sustainability concerns when caught in commercial volumes, and it is often better to use responsibly farmed fish. There are exciting developments in deep-water farming of fish which I believe will be the future for sourcing and supply of most of our seafood.

I have deliberately included recipes for cooking with carp and tilapia as these are some of the lesser-known farmed species, despite being the two largest in terms of world production and we are now seeing more of them for sale in supermarkets. As with salmon and trout, these should be readily available to buy from sustainable and responsibly farmed sources.

Sourcing any variety of fish can have a huge impact on the environment and species' viability, even land-farmed fish and prawns can be fed using sea-caught krill and other protein which can impact wild species by depriving them of their food supply. Choosing the right fish in terms of sustainability is difficult, there is a vast amount of information available for the latest views and opinions, but they do change regularly as more information becomes available and investment is made in research. A small local catch from a boat using a fishing line has a very different impact on fish stocks to that of a large fleet of offshore trawlers sweeping the ocean clean with nets that catch everything in their wake. Ultimately, the more you know, the better you can choose produce that has the least harmful effect on the environment we live in.

What I buy for home use is sustainable fish from supermarkets and I will buy more interesting and unusual fish from a local boat or a fishmonger with an understanding of how they were caught. And I would encourage you to do the same if you can.

Think about the flavours and textures of different species when you're looking for a fish to suit a recipe if you can't easily buy the variety listed for the recipe you want to cook.

Most flat fish will work well with any of the recipes on pages 93–105, so make the recipes using whichever variety is in season and available to you.

Fishcakes, curries, bouillabaisse and gumbo all use fish as an ingredient rather than the star of the dish, so most types of fish will work well in these recipes, in fact you can use pretty much any variety of fish, apart from very small fish that may disintegrate when cooked in these ways.

Squid and octopus cook in similar ways to each other, so try them with each other's recipes. It's a simple but effective approach.

For the shellfish recipes on pages 123–157, try using alternative types of shellfish; they'll all work well.

Ultimately, you should remember to always buy as fresh as you can: fish should have almost no aroma when you use it, just a hint of sea. Try not to overwork seafood when filleting and preparing it (see pages 57, 97, 128, 152 and 161); some fish, mackerel especially, will not take much handling before they start to fall apart. I recommend holding the fish with a kitchen cloth to limit the pressure and heat you apply with your hands while preparing seafood. Keep your seafood cool at all times before cooking. If you're not confident preparing fish, then ask your fishmonger to prepare it for you; if you want to learn ask them to show you how, they should be more than happy to demonstrate their skills.

Seafood flavours vary depending on seasons, where they've been caught and the age of the fish, so don't feel you must follow the recipe measurements religiously. Change the seasoning to your taste and always check the flavouring before you serve. Experiment as you become more confident in your own cooking at home and, above all, enjoy cooking and eating some great seafood.

BASIC STOCKS & SOUPS

The key to any good kitchen is a good stock, you can buy decent stocks but they'll only ever be a poor imitation of a stock you can make yourself. To make good stock the starting point is a *mirepoix* (a mixture of chopped onion, celery and carrots in two:one:one ratio by weight), which gives a depth of flavour to the stock. I've added a hint of tomato and citrus to these stocks as these go so well with seafood recipes.

Fish stocks should be made with gelatinous fish. Flat fish are great for this, also monkfish, hake, cod, etc., but don't bother with salmon or oily fish like mackerel. Trim gills and guts (after the fillets have been removed for cooking) and use them in stocks.

Prawns/shrimp or shellfish can be made into a stock on their own or added to a fish stock, but be careful as they can be very overpowering. Use scallop frills and the juices after cooking off any shellfish for your shellfish stocks.

The Fish Stock (opposite) is great for stews, soups and whenever the stock is being used for a sauce base. The Fish Consommé (a clear fish stock) requires a little more finesse and a lot more time to prepare but the resulting liquid is a joy to work with and I use it in the Rockpool Soup with Squid, Clams, Mussels, Seaweed & Samphire (page 124).

One thing to remember: never add salt to stock, never ever! Season what you make with it, not the stock. Different meals take different seasoning, so season towards the end of cooking and taste before serving. Bought stocks are usually mostly salt as most cooks tend to under season; trust your tastebuds when cooking and add the salt when you have made the finished dish.

FISH STOCK

PREPARE: **10 MINUTES** COOK: **1 HOUR**
MAKES: **2 LITRES/3½ PINTS**

4 brown onions, peeled and roughly chopped
8 carrots, thinly sliced
8 celery stalks, thinly sliced
2 tomatoes, cut into quarters
the peel of 1 lemon
2 litres/3½ pints cold water
1 kg/2 lbs. fish bones
100 g/1½ cups uncooked prawns/shrimp, shells on

Put all of the ingredients in a large pan set over a gentle–medium heat, bring to a low simmer and cook for 15 minutes. Reduce the heat and continue to cook for a further 45 minutes.

Pour the liquid through a fine mesh sieve/strainer into a jug/pitcher and discard the pulp.

SHELLFISH STOCK

PREPARE: **10 MINUTES** COOK: **1 HOUR**
MAKES: **2 LITRES/3½ PINTS**

4 brown onions, peeled and roughly chopped
8 carrots, thinly sliced
8 celery stalks, thinly sliced
2 tomatoes, cut into quarters
the peel of 1 lemon
2 litres/3½ pints cold water
300 ml/1¼ cups shellfish juices (or 200 g/7 oz. scallop frills)
200 g/3 cups uncooked prawns/shrimp, shells on

Put all of the ingredients in a large pan set over a gentle–medium heat, bring to a low simmer and cook for 15 minutes. Reduce the heat and continue to cook for a further 45 minutes.

Blend the mixture using a handheld electric blender, then pour the liquid through a fine mesh sieve/strainer into a jug/pitcher. Discard the pulp.

FISH CONSOMMÉ

PREPARE: **10 MINUTES** COOK: **3 HOURS**
MAKES: **1 LITRE/1¾ PINTS**

4 brown onions, peeled and roughly chopped
8 carrots, thinly sliced
8 celery stalks, thinly sliced
2 tomatoes, cut into quarters
the peel of 1 lemon
2 litres/3½ pints cold water
1 kg/2 lbs. fish bones

a sugar thermometer

Put all of the ingredients in a large pan set over a gentle–medium heat. Bring to a temperature of 80°C (175°F), testing with the sugar thermometer, and maintain this heat for 2 hours.

Check the flavour has fully infused and leave for another hour if not.

Carefully ladle off about 1 litre/1¾ pints of the liquid into a jug/pitcher without disturbing any sediment in the bottom of the pan. Discard the remainder or save for making a fish stock.

VEGETABLE STOCK

PREPARE: **10 MINUTES** COOK: **45 MINUTES**
MAKES: **2 LITRES/3½ PINTS**

4 brown onions, peeled and roughly chopped
8 carrots, thinly sliced
8 celery stalks, thinly sliced
2 tomatoes, cut into quarters
the peel of 1 lemon
2 litres/3½ pints cold water

Put all of the ingredients in a large pan set over a gentle heat, bring to a low simmer and cook for 45 minutes.

Pour the liquid through a fine mesh sieve/strainer into a jug/pitcher and discard the pulp.

FISH SOUP

PREPARE: **20 MINUTES** COOK: **15 MINUTES** SERVES: **4**

Fish soup (or shellfish soup) is a great appetizer and will tantalize the tastebuds for whatever dish is served next, or serve on its own with crusty bread for a light lunch. With careful knife skills the presentation of this dish is stunning and a classy start to a meal.

2 celery stalks

2 carrots

1 brown onion

2 litres/3½ pints Fish Stock (see page 11)

200 g/7 oz. white fish fillet (such as haddock, cod or whiting), diced into 1-cm/⅜-in. pieces

50 g/½ cup grated Gruyère cheese

a dash of Tabasco sauce

½ teaspoon salt

50 ml/3½ tablespoons double/heavy cream

SHELLFISH SOUP (OPTIONAL)

2 litres/3½ pints Shellfish Stock (see page 11)

200 g/7 oz. mussels, cooked and shelled

200 g/7 oz. clams, cooked and shelled

Peel and dice the vegetables into about 4-mm/⅛-in. pieces.

Put the diced vegetables in a large pan set over a gentle heat and pour over the stock. Bring the mixture to a low simmer and cook for 10 minutes.

Add the diced fish fillet and continue to simmer for another 5 minutes. Add the cheese, Tabasco and salt to taste. Pour in the cream and stir to combine. Sprinkle with black pepper and serve.

Variation: Try replacing the fish fillet with mussels and clams (you will need to cook the mussels and clams to extract the meat following the instructions on page 73), and replace fish stock with shellfish stock, and cook in the same way for a delicious shellfish version of this soup.

SALMON & TUNA

Salmon and tuna are probably the two most versatile and recognized fish species, so much so that they deserve their own chapter.

Both fish are delicious served raw or cooked and I have to confess to a love of good canned tuna and salmon, too. Try a few slices of fresh salmon or tuna with a little wasabi and soy sauce, so simple and so good to eat. Tuna steak, very different from the canned product we're all familiar with, is easy to cook and is a real delight to eat.

The recipes in this chapter range from a fun and simple Tuna & Anchovy Pizza (page 27) to a fairly complicated Salmon & Dill Pithivier (page 23) that is a brilliant dinner party dish. My family's favourite is Thai-flavoured Salmon Noodles (page 24) – it's easy to prepare in advance and quick to cook after the school run. Teriyaki Salmon (page 16) is sweet and sticky, delicious to eat and easy to make. It is a regular on my restaurant menu and at home; perfect for Spring when other varieties of fish can be in short supply.

Why not try curing salmon? I've included several suggestions but do play around with the flavours to create your own versions once you've mastered the curing process. It's surprisingly simple to home cure and at a huge cost saving by comparison to the prices charged for packaged cured salmon, and it looks amazing too.

TERIYAKI SALMON

PREPARE: **10 MINUTES** COOK: **20 MINUTES** SERVES: **4**

Teriyaki is a delicious sauce, made incredibly simply and it stores for weeks. The word refers to the sugar glaze (teri) and the cooking method of grilling/broiling the meat (yaki), so the idea is to cook the fish in the teriyaki sauce until it has reduced to a tasty, sticky glaze. The sauce works well with most fish and is sometimes used for meat too – pork or chicken work really well. I recommend serving the salmon with some steamed pak choi/bok choy and plain rice. Mirin or cooking rice wine is found in many supermarkets now. If you like this sauce I suggest buying larger bottles from an Asian supermarket or online and making a larger batch of the sauce to keep. Take care to only use a medium or low heat when cooking this dish as the sauce can catch and burn easily due to the high sugar content. Do not leave it cooking unsupervised.

100 g/generous ½ cup long-grain rice

a pinch of salt

4 salmon fillets (each about 120 g/4 oz.)

2 tablespoons sesame oil

2 heads of pak choi/bok choy, sliced in half

a 5-cm/2-in. piece of fresh ginger, peeled and finely grated

2 spring onions/scallions, thinly sliced

TERIYAKI SAUCE

200 ml/¾ cup mirin

50 ml/3½ tablespoons soy sauce

100 g/½ cup caster/granulated sugar

Begin by making the teriyaki sauce. Put the mirin and soy sauce together with the sugar in a small pan set over a gentle heat. Simmer for 2 minutes and stir until all the ingredients are combined. Remove from the heat and set aside.

Next, cook the rice. Bring 300 ml/1¼ cups of water to the boil in a saucepan set over a medium heat. Add the rice and salt, and bring back to the boil. Once boiling, take the pan off the heat, cover and set aside to allow the rice to cook for 15 minutes.

To prepare the salmon fillets, carefully remove the skin using a small sharp knife and check the flesh for any bones with your fingertips, removing and discarding any you find with fish tweezers.

Meanwhile, set a non-stick frying pan/skillet over a medium heat and pour in the oil. Heat until the oil just starts to smoke, then carefully place the salmon fillets in the pan. Cook until half of each fillet has coloured before adding the teriyaki sauce to the pan. Cover and simmer for 5 minutes. Carefully spoon over the teriyaki sauce, then remove the salmon using a fish slice. Transfer to a clean plate and cover with foil to keep warm.

Turn up the heat and reduce the remaining sauce for 2 minutes, until it has started to thicken.

Place the pak choi/bok choy cut-side down in the pan, cover and cook for 1 minute so that it just cooks in the steam.

To serve, strain the cooked rice and place a spoonful in each large bowl. Place some pak choi/bok choy on top, then the salmon. Sprinkle some of the grated ginger over the plate then add the sliced spring onions/scallion to finish.

CURED SALMON GRAVADLAX

PREPARE: **30 MINUTES** CURE: **24 HOURS** SERVES: **8–10**

Curing your own salmon is easy and a great discussion point. Here, I describe a basic salt and sugar cure as well as a few alternative flavour combinations, but experiment with flavours and try your own – beetroot/beet and vodka is a common cure for chefs to use, which looks stunning, if a little messy when making. Use the cured salmon in place of smoked salmon for recipes throughout the book. Although the curing process is traditionally used to allow fish to be stored, I advise you to use the prepared fish within four days of curing for best results. Buy the best salmon you can and have the fishmonger descale and pin-bone it for you. Gravadlax is a Nordic cured salmon, served with a dill sauce; try it with crusty bread and some hot, buttered new potatoes.

1 side of salmon (about 800 g/1¾ lbs.), descaled, pin-boned, with skin on

250 g/1¼ cups sea salt

250 g/1¼ cups caster/granulated sugar

GRAVADLAX CURE

a small bunch of fresh flat-leaf parsley, finely chopped

2 teaspoons ground coriander seeds

a bunch of fresh dill, finely chopped

freshly squeezed juice of 1 lemon

GRAVADLAX SAUCE

50 ml/3½ tablespoons white wine vinegar

80 g/⅓ cup muscovado sugar

60 g/4 tablespoons Dijon mustard

2 teaspoons vegetable oil

a bunch of fresh dill

TO SERVE

grated zest of 1 lemon or lime

a bunch of fresh dill, finely chopped

1 loaf rye bread, sliced

CITRUS CURE (OPTIONAL)

grated zest of 2 lemons

grated zest of 2 oranges

freshly squeezed juice of 1 lemon

VODKA CURE (OPTIONAL)

60 ml/4 tablespoons vodka

grated zest of 2 lemons

grated zest of 2 limes

Put the salt, sugar and gravadlax cure ingredients (or your choice of other cure) in a large mixing bowl and stir well to combine.

Stretch a piece of clingfilm/plastic wrap over a large plate and spread about one-third of the cure mixture over the top. Lay the salmon on top, skin-side down. Cover with the rest of the cure mixture, then bring up the clingfilm/plastic wrap around the salmon. Seal with a second piece of clingfilm/plastic wrap to form a tightly wrapped package.

Place the salmon on a large plate, then put another plate on top. Use several cans from your pantry as weights on top of the second plate and set in the fridge for 12 hours. After 12 hours, turn the salmon over and re-weight.

After 24 hours has passed, remove the salmon and rinse under cold water. Pat dry with a clean kitchen cloth or paper towels, then decorate the salmon with citrus zest and chopped fresh dill.

To make the gravadlax sauce, put all of the ingredients in a food processor and blitz for 2–3 minutes until well combined. Serve alongside the cured salmon gravadlax with sliced rye bread.

SALMON CAVIAR CANAPÉS

PREPARE: **30 MINUTES**   COOK: **10 MINUTES**   MAKES: **30**

Forget sturgeon caviar, for me the best roe money can buy is salmon – it's not as salty or as overtly fishy as true caviar, however, so if you like eating your salted anchovies by the can, you might want to save up for the real stuff. Salmon roe is stunning to look at and this recipe is for a simple canapé that will get you thinking of other uses for roe. Try using it in dishes as a garnish to add a visual and taste sparkle to any plate of seafood.

2 cooked beetroot/beets

1 focaccia loaf

olive oil, to drizzle

150 g/½ cup horseradish sauce

100 g/3½ oz. cured salmon (see page 19), thinly sliced

50 g/3½ tablespoons salmon roe

a small bunch of fresh dill

Preheat the oven to 180°C (350°F) Gas 4.

Thinly slice the beetroot/beets and cut into 2-cm/¾-in. squares.

Cut 6 thin slices of the focaccia and then cut into 2.5-cm/1-in. squares. Place on a a baking sheet and drizzle with a little olive oil. Bake in the preheated oven for 5 minutes, until crispy. Remove the focaccia from the oven and set aside to cool slightly.

Spread a little horseradish sauce on each focaccia square, then place a square of beetroot/beet on top, followed by a generous slice of cured salmon. Dress each one with a few roe and some dill tops and serve.

SALMON & DILL PITHIVIER

PREPARE: **40 MINUTES**   COOK: **15 MINUTES**   SERVES: **4**

A Pithivier is a thing of delight! Traditionally a puff pastry parcel filled with almond paste and served as a dessert, they are now commonly made as a savoury dish. Think a delicious pie with buttery puff pastry and the wonderful combination of salmon and dill. If you purchase sides of salmon, save the offcuts in a bag in the freezer and make this dish when you have enough pieces. I use sea beetroot/beet leaves in the restaurant but have used spinach here as it is a lot easier to get hold of.

a small bunch of fresh dill, finely chopped, stems discarded

400 g/14 oz. salmon, diced into bite-sized pieces

2 pinches of sea salt flakes

250 g/9 oz. readymade puff pastry

1 egg, beaten

1 teaspoon English/hot mustard

a handful of fresh spinach leaves

mixed green salad, to serve

a 6.5-cm/2½-in. round cookie cutter

Preheat the oven to 180°C (350°F) Gas 4.

Mix the dill and salmon together with a couple of pinches of sea salt in a large mixing bowl. Set aside.

Roll out the pastry on a cool, lightly floured surface to about a 4-mm/⅛-in. thickness. You should be able to cut 8 circles from the pastry using the round cookie cutter.

Cut four squares of baking parchment slightly bigger than the pastry circles and place four of the circles on them. Glaze the outer edges of these circles with the beaten egg to a width of about 2.5 cm/1 in. from the edge. Put ¼ teaspoon of mustard in the unglazed area in the middle of each and spread, before placing several spinach leaves on top to form a base. Place one-quarter of the salmon and dill mixture on top to form a mound.

Gently stretch the centre of the unused pastry discs then carefully cover the mounds, sealing the pastry at the glazed edges. Use a fork to squeeze the edges together and trim off any excess pastry using the cookie cutter.

Glaze the pastry with the beaten egg and once the glaze has dried use a sharp knife to carefully score a spiral pattern on the tops of each Pithivier.

Transfer each Pithivier on its square of baking parchment to a baking sheet and bake in the preheated oven for 15 minutes.

Serve immediately with a mixed green salad.

THAI-FLAVOURED SALMON NOODLES

PREPARE: **30 MINUTES** COOK: **10 MINUTES** SERVES: **4**

Salmon may not be a traditional fish for Thai cooking but it handles the robustness of Thai flavours better than most fish. It's all about balancing sweet and sour, spice and salt, so do adjust the balance of flavours depending how intense you like them. I'm not a fan of much chilli/chile heat so this recipe is written with less than you might traditionally find. Don't be scared to add more heat by adding extra chilli/chile, or by substituting green with red, but increase the salt (Nam pla), sour (lime) and sweet (tamarind) flavourings as well to maintain a good balance. This recipe is intentionally light but for a richer flavour, use a can of coconut milk instead of just water for the sauce. I like to slice the vegetables for a pop of flavour and texture but you can use the same mixture and grind them using a pestle and mortar to make a paste if you prefer. As with most Asian cooking this dish takes time to prepare and minutes to cook so you can prepare everything well in advance and keep the ingredients in the fridge until dinner time. Oil your hands lightly or wear latex gloves when preparing chillies/chiles... and never rub your eyes until your fingers have been thoroughly cleaned afterwards!

4 salmon fillets (each about 120 g/4 oz.)

300 g/8 oz. flat rice noodles

SAUCE

400 ml/14 oz. canned coconut milk (optional)

50 g/¼ cup tamarind paste

1 teaspoon fish sauce (Nam Pla)

grated zest and freshly squeezed juice of 2 limes

2 lemongrass stalks, bruised and thinly sliced

2 green chillies/chiles, thinly sliced

2 red Thai chillies/chiles, thinly sliced

2 garlic cloves, peeled and thinly sliced

1 tablespoon grated fresh ginger (or 2 tablespoons Galangal ginger, if available)

a small bunch of fresh coriander/cilantro, thinly sliced, leaves reserved to serve

First, prepare the salmon fillets. Carefully remove the skin using a small sharp knife and check the flesh for any bones with your fingertips, removing and discarding any you find with fish tweezers.

Pour 600 ml/2½ cups of water (or the coconut milk with 200 ml/¾ cup of water if you prefer a richer sauce) into a large saucepan or pot. Add the sauce ingredients, stir and set over a low–medium heat. Simmer gently for 2–3 minutes to allow the flavours to infuse.

Add the noodles to the pan then carefully place the salmon on top. Cover with a lid and continue to simmer for 3–4 minutes (or up to 6 minutes if you want the salmon to be well cooked).

Carefully lift the salmon pieces out of the pan using a fish slice. Transfer to a clean plate and cover with foil to keep warm, then set aside.

Stir the noodles and sauce before transferring to serving bowls. Place the salmon on top, dress with coriander/cilantro leaves and serve.

TUNA & ANCHOVY PIZZA

PREPARE: **2 HOURS 25 MINUTES** COOK: **25 MINUTES** SERVES: **4**

The satisfaction of making your own pizza bases can't be underestimated and it is probably easier than you think. You can even make a batch of the pizzas, wrap and freeze them.

180 ml/¾ cup warm water

5 g/¼ oz. fast-action dried yeast

300 g/2⅓ cups strong bread flour

1 teaspoon salt

40 ml/3 tablespoons extra virgin olive oil, plus extra to drizzle

TOPPINGS

60 g/4 tablespoons tomato purée/paste

200 g/1½ cups grated mozzarella cheese

200 g/2 cups grated cheddar cheese

50 g/½ cup grated Parmesan cheese

50 g/½ cup canned anchovies in oil

160 g/⅔ cup canned tuna in spring water

1 red onion, peeled and finely chopped

a small bunch of fresh tarragon

4 baking sheets, oiled

To make the pizza dough, combine the warm water, yeast, flour, salt and oil in a large mixing bowl. Bring the ingredients together into one ball using the tips of your fingers. Turn out onto an oiled worktop and with the base of your hand stretch and knead the dough for 10 minutes.

When the dough is a smooth and consistent texture, it's ready to prove. Drizzle a little oil into the base of a large bowl, oil the ball of dough, and put in the bowl. Cover with a clean kitchen cloth and put the bowl somewhere warm (an airing cupboard is ideal for this) for 1½ hours.

Preheat the oven to 220°C (425°F) Gas 7.

Once proved, the dough should be at least twice its original size. Gently turn it out onto an oiled surface and knead the dough gently to knock out the air. Divide it into four portions. Put each of the pieces of dough onto a separate prepared baking sheet and stretch the dough with your fingertips until it is about 5 mm/¼ in. thick. Don't worry about making the base completely even as thinner or thicker areas add to the flavour and texture of the finished pizza.

Bake each base (one at a time depending on the size of your oven) in the preheated oven for 6 minutes. Remove them from the baking sheets and put back in the oven, directly on the oven shelf, to cook for another 3 minutes.

To finish, spread 15 g/1 tablespoon of tomato purée/paste on each pizza base and sprinkle evenly with the cheeses. Place the anchovies evenly across each pizza and do the same with the tuna and the red onion. Return the pizzas to the oven, directly on the oven shelf, for 10 minutes.

Sprinkle with freshly chopped tarragon, slice and serve immediately.

Tip: To freeze the pizzas cook for only 6 minutes of the final cooking time, then remove from the oven and set aside to cool completely. Place in a large sealable bag and freeze. To cook from frozen, preheat the oven to 220°C (425°F) Gas 7 and cook, directly on the oven shelf, for 6 minutes.

GRILLED TUNA NIÇOISE SALAD

PREPARE: **30 MINUTES** COOK: **10 MINUTES** SERVES: **4**

Salad Niçoise, if you're English, is made with canned tuna, boiled eggs and olives; if you're from other countries it can have anchovies instead of tuna or fresh tuna steak and some have potatoes and lettuce leaves too. All Niçoise seem to have boiled eggs, olives, tomatoes, garlic and capers, so mine does, too. My Niçoise does not try to be perfectly authentic but instead aims to capture the essence of the salad. I use anchovies and serve with some waxy new potatoes and a tuna steak to make a full meal.

4 hard-boiled/hard-cooked eggs

salt and ground white pepper, to season

4 ripe red tomatoes, cut into wedges

a pinch of caster/granulated sugar

1 celery stalk, thinly sliced

50 g/½ cup pitted black olives, sliced into rounds

200 g/1½ cups small waxy new potatoes, boiled

½ cucumber

2 teaspoons capers

8 canned anchovies, sliced in half lengthwise

4 spring onions/scallions, thinly sliced at an angle

a small bunch of fresh marjoram

4 tuna steaks (each about 120 g/4 oz.)

oil, to coat

PESTO

100 g/¾ cup pine nuts

2 garlic cloves, peeled

a small bunch of fresh basil

freshly squeezed juice of ½ lemon

a pinch of salt

olive oil, to drizzle

Begin by making the pesto; put the pine nuts, garlic and half of the basil in a food processor and pulse until combined but still with some texture. Add half of the lemon juice and the salt, and taste. Pour in a little oil to loosen the mixture, then add more basil and lemon as needed and pulse a couple more times, until the pesto can just be poured.

Next, prepare the salad. Peel and wedge the eggs, and season with a tiny amount of salt and white pepper. Sprinkle a tiny amount of sugar over the tomatoes and set aside for 5 minutes. Arrange the remaining ingredients except for the marjoram and tuna steaks on serving plates. Sprinkle with crushed marjoram leaves and drizzle each salad with a generous portion of the pesto.

Preheat a ridged stove-top grill pan over a high heat. Lightly oil the tuna steaks and season with a little salt. Place carefully on the pan and turn after 2–3 minutes, when the tuna is just charred and griddle lines are formed. Cook for another couple of minutes on the other side and serve on top of the salad.

TUNA STEAK WITH A WASABI CRUST

PREPARE: **10 MINUTES**   COOK: **10 MINUTES**   SERVES: **4**

Tuna and wasabi work so well together. This is simplicity itself to make and stores in the fridge easily so is a great treat to make in advance and ideal served as an appetizer, as it is here.

250 g/9 oz. tuna steak

salt, to season

sesame oil, for frying, plus a little extra to serve

1 tablespoon wasabi powder

1–2 teaspoons soy sauce

4 nori sheets

200 g/3½ cups beansprouts

1 lime, peeled and roughly chopped

chilli/hot red pepper flakes

Trim the tuna steak into cubes about 5 cm/2 in. wide and season with a small pinch of salt.

Set a non-stick frying pan/skillet over a medium heat and pour in a little oil. When the oil starts to smoke, place the tuna carefully in the pan. Cook for 30–45 seconds on each side to lightly caramelize but not cook all the way through – the tuna should be rare and cooked no more than 1 cm/⅜ in. into the meat. Remove from the heat, set aside to cool, then chill in the fridge.

Meanwhile, make a paste, the consistency of double/heavy cream with the wasabi powder and soy sauce. Once the seared tuna has chilled, roll it in the paste. Cover the tuna in the nori (you might find it easier to crush the nori sheets to a powder and roll the wasabi-coated tuna in it).

Toss the beansprouts in a little sesame oil and arrange on serving plates with a little of the chopped lime. Slice the tuna thinly and set on top of the beansprout salad. Sprinkle with chilli/hot red pepper flakes and serve.

Tip: You can use this recipe to make some interesting and unusual canapés. Take a rice cracker and place a few beansprouts on top of it, then add a small piece of lime, a piece of tuna and a couple of chilli/hot red pepper flakes on top for a delicious bite-sized portion.

FRESHWATER FISH

We don't eat nearly enough freshwater fish; in the United Kingdom they are seen as sport fish and usually put back in the water once they've been caught. For over 2000 years in China and other Southeast Asian countries carp were traditionally farmed in rice fields. In a symbiotic relationship, they would grow in the flooded fields as the rice grew, grazing on the weeds, helping the rice crop. When the fields were drained to cultivate the rice, the farmer had wonderful fish to eat and to sell.

The recipes in this chapter make the most of the wonderful flavours of freshwater fish and eel, from a grand sharing platter of carp cooked in a Southeast Asian-style masterstock (page 39), to the western flavours of a Smoked Eel, Beetroot & Horseradish Salad (page 43). Trout en Papillote (page 37) is a dish I've served for years in my restaurants, collecting trout from a local farm, we often serve it within an hour of the trout being caught.

Tilapia are becoming a more common fish variety found on supermarket shelves, as farming and acceptance of them increases. Like carp, tilapia can be farmed using vegetable protein, so farming them has a minimal environmental impact. Tilapia and carp can accommodate strong flavours well, like in the Soy & Ginger Tilapia recipe on page 40.

TROUT PÂTÉ

PREPARE: **5 MINUTES** COOK: **15 MINUTES** SERVES: **4**

Trout has a delicious but very delicate flavour, which is easily overpowered by other ingredients, so it's important to keep your dish simple with well-balanced flavours. Here, I've used a small amount of horseradish to give a hint of heat and a little citrus for sharpness.

4 trout fillets (each about 120 g/4 oz.), deboned and skinned

freshly squeezed juice of 1 lemon, plus wedges to serve

50 ml/3½ tablespoons double/heavy cream

1 teaspoon horseradish sauce

salt and ground white pepper

melba toast (or water crackers), to serve

freshly ground black pepper, to serve (optional)

To prepare the trout fillets, carefully remove the skin using a small sharp knife and check the flesh for any bones with your fingertips, removing and discarding any you find with fish tweezers.

Place the trout in a large saucepan, add the lemon juice and enough water to just cover them. Set the pan over a gentle heat and bring to a low simmer. Poach for 5 minutes before carefully removing the trout from the poaching liquor using a slotted spoon or fish slice.

Put the poached trout in a food processor and set the liquor aside.

Add the double/heavy cream, horseradish sauce, a pinch of salt and white pepper, then blend to the consistency of a smooth paste. Add a little of the poaching liquor if the mixture is too dry and blend again.

Press the paste into ramekins, cover and chill in the fridge for at least 1 hour.

Serve the pâté simply with melba toast or water crackers and lemon wedges on the side. Season with a little extra black pepper if desired.

TROUT EN PAPILLOTE

PREPARE: **10 MINUTES**   COOK: **35 MINUTES**   SERVES: **4**

Cooking fish doesn't get much simpler than this: stuff the cavity with a few aromatic ingredients, seal in paper and bake. Baking in paper is a very effective way to maintain moisture and infuse flavours into the fish. This recipe uses lime, lemon grass and ginger to give the trout, which can otherwise be a fairly flavourless fish, a boost. I serve it with potatoes, lemon and fennel for a satisfying and light meal.

600 g/1¼ lbs. new potatoes, cut in half

1 fennel bulb, thinly sliced into 15–20 slices

1 lemon, thinly sliced into 15–20 slices

vegetable oil, to drizzle

1 teaspoon salt

4 whole trout (each about 450 g/1 lb.), gutted

2 limes, cut into 8 wedges

2 lemon grass stalks, thinly sliced

a 7.5-cm/3-in. piece of fresh ginger, peeled and thinly sliced across the grain

Preheat the oven to 180°C (350°F) Gas 4.

Boil the potatoes in a pan of salted water for 10–15 minutes until just soft.

Meanwhile, stuff the cavity of each of the fish with equal amounts of lime, lemon grass and ginger. Roll the fish in baking parchment, tucking the parchment around the ends of the fish.

Arrange the sliced fennel and lemon and the boiled potatoes in a deep ovenproof dish. Drizzle with oil and the salt and toss to combine. Roast in the preheated oven for 20 minutes.

Place the fish parcels in the oven on top of the potato mixture and bake for 20 minutes. Check the temperature of the fish by using a meat thermometer before removing from the oven, it should be 60°C (170°F) at the thickest part.

Serve the trout on top of the potato, lemon and fennel mixture in its wrapping. Carefully unwrap the fish at the table, releasing the wonderful aromas and allowing any juices to soak into the vegetables beneath.

SOUTHEAST ASIAN MASTERSTOCK POACHED CARP

PREPARE: **10 MINUTES**   COOK: **1 HOUR 10 MINUTES**   SERVES: **6-8**

A masterstock is a wonderful thing. In many Southeast Asian countries it is revered and is the basis for a restaurant's entire menu – they are traditionally kept for long periods of time. I don't recommend keeping the stock unfrozen for more than a few days in the fridge (or a month or so in the freezer) but it is worth the time taken to make it a day or two in advance and allowing the flavours to infuse in that time. The ingredients should all be easily found in an Asian supermarket.

1 large carp (about 2 kg/4½ lbs.) descaled, gutted and trimmed

300 g/1½ cups long-grain rice

a pinch of salt

4 pak choi/bok choy, halved

2 spring onions/scallions, thinly sliced on an angle

1 lime

drinking rice wine or sake, to serve

MASTERSTOCK

2 litres/3½ pints Fish Stock (see page 11)

100 ml/⅓ cup dark soy sauce

200 ml/¾ cup tamari soy sauce

150 ml/⅔ cup rice wine

50 g/¼ cup brown sugar

2 star anise

1 teaspoon fennel seeds

1 cardamom pod

the peel of 1 orange

1 teaspoon Sichuan peppercorns

1 Bird's eye chilli/chile, sliced

2 teaspoons grated galangal (or 1 teaspoon grated fresh ginger)

2-4 teaspoons fish sauce (Nam Pla), to taste

In an extra-large pan (large enough to hold the fish), pour the fish stock and add the other masterstock ingredients except for the fish sauce. Set over a gentle heat and bring to a low simmer for 30 minutes. Taste the masterstock and add the fish sauce one teaspoon at a time to balance the flavours as required. Or alternatively add the following seasonings: if it's too hot add more sugar, too sweet add more wine, too salty add stock and sugar. The skill of this dish is balancing the flavours of the masterstock to a combination you like; it should be a mild balance of sweet, salty, savoury and heat.

Once you are happy with the masterstock, cut three diagonal lines in each side of the carp and carefully place in the stock. Keep over a gentle heat with the carp submerged in the warm but not simmering stock – about 85°C (185°F) ideally – and cook for 40 minutes to allow the flavours to infuse.

Meanwhile, cook the rice. Bring 600 ml/2½ cups of water to the boil in a saucepan set over a medium heat. Add the rice and salt, and bring back to the boil. Once boiling, take the pan off the heat, cover and set aside to allow the rice to cook for 15 minutes. Cook the pak choi/bok choy in a covered steamer set over the rice, or boil in water for 2 minutes in a separate pan.

Place the rice in a large bowl and sprinkle with spring onions/scallions. Serve the fish on a platter with the steamed pak choi/bok choy surrounding it and the lime squeezed over just before serving for fragrance and flavour. A little warmed rice wine or sake is the perfect accompaniment to this dish.

SOY & GINGER TILAPIA

PREPARE: **20 MINUTES** COOK: **10 MINUTES** SERVES: **4**

Tilapia is a fantastic base for recipes, it lends itself well to Southeast Asian flavours and this recipe is a good example. I love the combination of garlic, ginger and soy; build on this to your own taste using spring onions/ scallions like I have, or substitute chillies/ chiles, lemon grass, miso, kaffir lime or any combination you feel like – have fun and experiment! I use Chinese cabbage but you can swap it for pak choi/bok choy or lettuce if you struggle to find it.

vegetable oil, for frying

2 tablespoons sesame oil

the leaves of 1 Chinese cabbage

4 tilapia fillets (each about 200 g/7 oz.), skinned and deboned

a 6.5-cm/2½-in. piece of fresh ginger, peeled and grated

4 garlic cloves, peeled and thinly sliced

freshly squeezed juice of 1 lime, plus wedges to serve

light soy sauce

a small bunch of spring onions/scallions, thinly sliced on a diagonal

1–2 teaspoons caster/granulated sugar

Cover the base of a large, heavy-based, non-stick frying pan/skillet with vegetable oil to a depth of about 2 mm/¹⁄₁₆ in. and set over a medium heat. The pan is warm enough to cook in when a piece of garlic sizzles, but doesn't burn, when dropped into it.

Add the sesame oil and carefully place about 8 cabbage leaves in the pan. Fry for a couple of minutes until just starting to crisp. Remove the cabbage and arrange on pre-warmed plates ready for the tilapia.

Carefully place the tilapia fillets in the pan, use the flat of a fish slice to hold them flat for a few seconds if they curl in the heat, then cook for 2–3 minutes, until the tilapia is just starting to caramelize and brown on the bottom (it should be nearly cooked through on the top at this point).

Take the pan off the heat and add the ginger and garlic; this should sizzle and cook fairly quickly. Very carefully, add the lime juice and a few teaspoons of soy sauce – this will take the temperature in the pan down and create an wonderful aroma. Spoon the oil, garlic and ginger over the top of the tilapia to finish the cooking, then sprinkle over the spring onions/scallions.

Place the tilapia on the cooked cabbage, stir the sugar into the pan juices, to taste, and spoon the contents of the pan over the tilapia to serve.

SMOKED EEL, BEETROOT & HORSERADISH SALAD

PREPARE: **30 MINUTES** COOK: **2 MINUTES** SERVES: **4**

I spent childhood mornings in New Zealand tracking eels as they moved across dew-covered grass to find new sources of water. They are incredibly hardy creatures that have sadly been over-fished. Once a food for the poor, eel has become rare and it is important to find a supplier of sustainable eel. It is worth seeking out though as eel has a delicious and unique flavour.
In London's East End they were traditionally boiled with vinegar, chilli/chile, lemon and nutmeg, then reduced to a jelly/gelatin. This recipe uses a small amount of smoked eel with vinegary beetroot/beet and hot horseradish as a nod to the traditional flavours that work so well with eel.

1 Little Gem/Bibb lettuce

50 g/3½ tablespoons hot horseradish sauce

50 g/1 cup wild rocket/arugula leaves

50 g/1 cup pea shoots

50 g/3 tablespoons finely grated pickled beetroot/beets

200 g/7 oz. smoked eel

nutmeg, for grating

DRESSING

100 ml/⅓ cup first-press rapeseed oil

20 ml/1½ tablespoons cider vinegar

1 teaspoon Dijon mustard

freshly squeezed juice of 1 lemon

1 teaspoon runny honey

a pinch of salt

Arrange 3 lettuce leaves each on serving plates.

On each leaf place ½ teaspoon of horseradish sauce and spread it a little. Arrange a few rocket/arugula leaves and pea shoots on top with a little beetroot/beet. Finally lay over a few pieces of eel

Make the dressing by placing all of the ingredients in a small bottle, sealing with a lid and shaking vigorously.

Pour over the dressing, then finely grate a little nutmeg over the top before serving. Use your fingers to roll up the individual lettuce leaves and eat these little eel parcels whole.

SMALL FISH

This chapter features a wonderful variety of fish, from strongly flavoured varieties like anchovy and sardines to the more subtle flavours of mackerel.

The first relaxation of Sunday trading laws in the United Kingdom was put in place specifically to allow mackerel to be sold in perfect condition in pre-refrigeration days, which gives us an insight into the correct treatment of mackerel: they must be sold or bought, eaten and prepared absolutely fresh.

Small fish are often cooked to preserve them. Recipes such as Soused Herrings (page 46) or Potted Smoked Mackerel (page 50) are fabulous ways to preserve the fish for days and can be made with any small fish you are able to source, whereas recipes such as Barbecue Mackerel with Tomatoes & Onions (page 53) and Mackerel Ceviche (page 49) should only use the very freshest of fish.

Mackerel and gooseberry is a classic flavour combination where the oily mackerel is paired with a sharp gooseberry flavour to create a balanced and tasty dish. Stargazy Pie (page 67) is a West Country classic, and makes a wonderful centrepiece for a dinner party. Although one of the most versatile small fish it's not all about mackerel, some of my favourite recipes use other small fish, such as Whitebait Fritters (page 58), Anchovy & Potato Gratin (page 63) and Pan-fried Sprats with Aioli (page 60).

SOUSED HERRINGS

PREPARE: **1 HOUR 15 MINUTES**
COOK: **10 MINUTES** MAKES: **8**

Soused herrings are a traditional part of a sharing platter. Serve them with cold cured meats and cheeses for a dramatic centrepiece, shared appetizer or canapés. Substitute two of the herring fillets for a mackerel fillet for a tasty light lunch and serve with some new potatoes.

100 ml/⅓ cup white wine vinegar

2 small red chillies/chiles, thinly sliced

50 g/¼ cup caster/granulated sugar

1 small brown onion, peeled and finely diced

8 herring fillets (each about 120 g/4 oz.), cleaned

1 teaspoon black peppercorns

BUTTERED NEW POTATOES (OPTIONAL)

300 g/11 oz. new potatoes, boiled

50 g/3½ tablespoons butter, melted

a small bunch of fresh flat-leaf parsley, chopped

a baking sheet, lined with baking parchment

Put the vinegar, chillies/chiles, sugar, onion and black pepper with 100 ml/⅓ cup of water in a large frying pan/skillet set over a medium heat. Stir until the sugar has dissolved.

Carefully place the herring fillets, skin-side up in the pan and heat until bubbles just start to appear in the liquor. Simmer for 3 minutes to allow the herring to cook through. Remove each fillet from the pan using a fish slice and place skin-side up, on the prepared baking sheet.

Increase the heat and bring the liquor to a rolling boil for a few minutes to reduce the volume by half. Pour the sauce over the herring and chill in the fridge for at least 1 hour.

Toss the boiled new potatoes in the melted butter with chopped parsley and serve alongside the chilled soused herrings. Decorate with the chilli/chile and onion from the sauce.

Tip: Soused herrings can also be enjoyed on their own with grated carrot, cucumber and served on lettuce leaves.

MACKEREL CEVICHE

PREPARE: **10 MINUTES**   CURE: **30 MINUTES**   SERVES: **4**

This really colourful dish looks amazing and requires no cooking (the acid in the fruit 'cooks' the fish). It is a great alternative for those who aren't quite ready to try sushi.

4 mackerel fillets (each about 100 g/
3½ oz.), deboned

grated zest and freshly squeezed juice
of 1 orange, 1 lime and 1 lemon, plus
1 lime and 1 lemon, cut into wedges

2 medium–hot red chillies/chiles, thinly
sliced

100 g/2 cups mixed salad leaves

a small bunch of fresh coriander/cilantro

Put the mackerel in a large dish. Grate and squeeze the orange, lime and lemon over the mackerel, then add the chillies/chiles. Gently spread the ingredients over the mackerel evenly, cover and set in the fridge for at least 30 minutes or up to 2 hours.

While the mackerel is 'cooking', prepare your salad, adding finely chopped coriander/cilantro and divide between serving plates.

Remove the mackerel from the liquor and place on top of the salad. Dress the plates with wedges of lime and lemon and serve.

POTTED SMOKED MACKEREL

PREPARE: **10 MINUTES**   COOK: **30 MINUTES**   SERVES: **4**

This is an ideal appetizer and a great dinner party dish. It can be made in advance and I love the smokiness combined with the heat of Tabasco. My recipe uses a fork to create a coarse texture, but you can use a food processor to achieve a smoother finish, or turn it into a pâté.

4 smoked mackerel fillets (each about 100 g/3½ oz.), deboned

freshly squeezed juice of ½ lemon

a pinch of salt and pepper

50 ml/3½ tablespoons double/heavy cream

a good few glugs of Tabasco (to taste)

1 teaspoon horseradish sauce

1 spring onion/scallion, sliced

100 ml/7 tablespoons butter

TO SERVE

16–20 melba toasts

a large handful fresh rocket/arugula

the seeds of 1 pomegranate

Place all of the ingredients except the butter in a large mixing bowl and use a fork to mix and mash everything together. Press the mixture into ramekins and set aside.

Melt the butter in a pan set over a medium heat and spoon over the top of the mackerel while still warm. This will form a light seal. Set aside to cool before chilling in the fridge for at least 30 minutes.

Serve the mackerel with melba toast, a few pomegranate seeds and a simple rocket/arugula salad.

BARBECUE MACKEREL WITH TOMATOES & ONIONS

PREPARE: **30 MINUTES** COOK: **10 MINUTES** SERVES: **4**

Barbecued mackerel is the taste of summer to me. This recipe is full of Mediterranean flavours and is easy to prepare in advance, ready to be placed on the barbecue and cooked. A little aniseed-flavoured Pernod thrown into the mix lifts this simple dish to something special.

8 medium tomatoes, each cut into 4 wedges

4 garlic cloves, peeled and thinly sliced

2 brown onions, peeled and roughly chopped

1 orange (bell) pepper, finely diced

50 ml/3½ tablespoons Pernod (or other aniseed-based liqueur)

salt and freshly ground black pepper

4 whole large mackerel (each about 170 g/6 oz.), cleaned and gutted

2 lemons, cut in half to serve

Begin by cutting four pieces of baking parchment about the same length as your fish and four pieces of foil a little larger than that. Place each piece of foil beneath the baking parchment and set aside.

Put the tomatoes, garlic, onions, and (bell) pepper with the Pernod in a large mixing bowl. Add a generous pinch of salt and pepper and mix together.

Place each fish on top of the pieces of baking parchment and foil, and cover with about a quarter of the tomato and onion mixture. Roll the paper and foil around the fish and seal by crimping the edges. Set in a fridge for a few hours to marinate.

When ready to cook, preheat a grill plate on the barbecue before placing the mackerel packages on top. Cook with the lid closed for 5 minutes, then carefully open the packages and cook for a further 5 minutes with the lid open to reduce the amount of liquid in the packages.

Serve straight from the barbecue, each with ½ lemon.

Tip: Barbecue temperatures can vary so alter the cooking times to suit and check that the meat is fully cooked before serving. If you have smoking chips, add them for the final 5 minutes of cooking time with the lid closed to make a wonderful smoky, tomato sauce.

MACKEREL KEDGEREE

PREPARE: **15 MINUTES** COOK: **25 MINUTES** SERVES: **4**

Originating in India as a breakfast dish called 'khichdi', kedgeree was brought back to the United Kingdom in Victorian times and modified as part of the Anglo-Indian cuisine of the time. It is a fish and curried rice brunch dish and there are few better morning-after meals to be had. Although traditionally cooked with smoked haddock, I like to use smoked mackerel as I prefer the colour and flavour but do try it with any smoked fish. Use a good-quality masala spice blend or make your own following the method used for my Goan Fish Curry on page 70.

vegetable oil, for frying

1 brown onion, peeled and diced

2 teaspoon garam masala (or Masala Spice Blend, page 70)

1 teaspoon turmeric powder

200 g/1½ cup long-grain rice

a pinch of salt

4 hard-boiled/hard-cooked eggs

50 g/⅓ cup frozen peas

2 red chillies/chiles, thinly sliced

a small bunch of fresh flat-leaf parsley

2 smoked mackerel fillets, flaked

50 ml/3½ tablespoons double/heavy cream

Add just enough oil to cover the base of a medium saucepan and set over a medium heat. Add the onion, garam masala and turmeric and heat for a couple of minutes before adding the rice. Stir to coat the rice in oil and spice, then add 400 ml/1⅔ cups of water and the salt. Bring to a simmer, then take the pan off the heat, cover and set aside to allow the rice to cook for 15 minutes.

Peel and wedge the boiled eggs and set aside.

Once the rice is cooked, return to a gentle heat and stir in the frozen peas. Add the chilli/chile and parsley, reserving some for decoration, before finally adding the flaked mackerel and cream. Carefully stir all of the ingredients together until evenly mixed and hot.

Transfer the kedgeree to a large casserole dish, decorate with the wedges of egg and a sprinkling of parsley and serve at the table.

Tip: In India, where the original dish kedgeree dish khichdi is still served it is traditional to serve it with a spiced yogurt drink, which is also sometimes stirred through. Try this kedgeree with a little plain yogurt stirred through just before serving to add an interesting sourness to the dish – it also serves to lessen the heat of the chilli/chile in the dish if, like me, you don't like too much chilli/chile heat.

MACKEREL BURGER WITH GOOSEBERRY SAUCE

PREPARE: **10 MINUTES**   COOK: **30 MINUTES**   MAKES: **4**

The oiliness of mackerel balances well with a tart sauce and a classic partner is gooseberry, especially as they tend to come into season as the mackerel becomes plentiful. If gooseberries are out of season, then try this dish with a horseradish or hollandaise sauce.

200 g/2 cups gooseberries, cut in half

70 g/⅓ cup caster/granulated sugar

100 g/7 tablespoons butter

4 whole mackerel (each about 170 g/ 6 oz.), filleted and deboned

4 brioche buns (or brioche finger rolls), sliced in half

80 g/1½ cups watercress

a pinch of salt and black pepper

Begin by making the sauce. Put the gooseberries in a small saucepan with the sugar and 100 ml/⅓ cup of water set over a gentle heat. Cover and cook for about 15 minutes, until the gooseberries are soft. Blend the mixture using a handheld electric blender, then pour the liquid through a fine-mesh sieve/strainer into a jug/pitcher. Discard the pulp and store in the fridge.

Put the butter in a large frying pan/skillet set over a medium heat. When the butter is foaming, carefully add the mackerel fillets skin side up and cook for 3–4 minutes, until cooked through.

To serve, place a small handful of watercress in each roll, then a generous dollop of gooseberry sauce and finally, two mackerel fillets. Season with salt and pepper to taste.

HOW TO FILLET SMALL & ROUND FISH

1 Hold the fish using a kitchen cloth (if preferred) and cut around the back of the head to the backbone. For larger fish, do this in a V-shape.

2 Cut the fillet away from the bones by scoring down the back of the body.

3 With the blade underneath the fillet cut the fillet away in a clean sweep.

4 Check for pin bones and remove with tweezers. Repeat for the other fillet. For small fish it is often easier to cut the pin bones away by carefully cutting a thin V-shape down the centre of the fillet, removing them all at once.

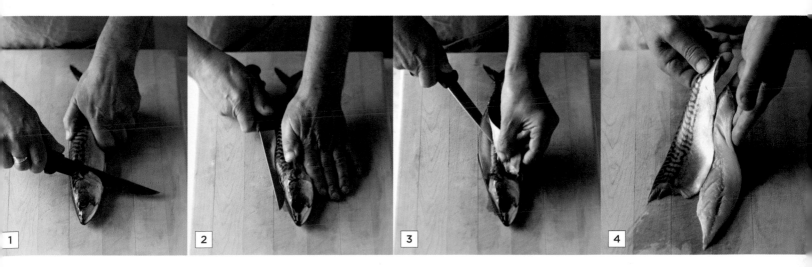

WHITEBAIT FRITTERS

PREPARE: **10 MINUTES**   COOK: **10 MINUTES**   SERVES: **2**

Whitebait are a delicacy and a delight when treated with respect when cooked. Whitebait fritters are a classic New Zealand dish and this is my take on them. As a kid in Auckland, New Zealand, whitebait were the answer to my lack of pocket money; we used to catch them by the shoal in handheld nets off the local wharf and sell them – one decent netful would keep me in sweets for a week. 'Whitebait' refers to the micro-fry of several small species of fish, herrings and sprats being the more common types. In the United Kingdom, whitebait are larger but still served whole so the recipe here is not a true fritter, but just as delicious.

200 g/1²⁄₃ cups plain/all-purpose flour

1 egg plus 1 egg yolk

200 g/³⁄₄ cup milk

salt and freshly ground black pepper

150 g/5 oz. whitebait/smelt (or micro-fry whitebait)

15 g/1 tablespoon butter

vegetable oil, for frying

mayonnaise, to serve

½ lemon, cut into wedges to serve

Sift the flour into a large mixing bowl and add the egg and egg yolk. Stir well, then slowly add all of the milk, stirring as you do – you should end up with a thick batter. Add a generous pinch of salt and black pepper and mix through. Now add the whitebait and carefully fold them through the mixture.

Put the butter and enough vegetable oil to just cover the base in a frying pan/skillet and set over a medium heat until the butter is foaming.

If the whitebait are larger than micro-fry (as pictured), carefully place the battered whitebait in the pan and cook for 3–4 minutes until golden brown, turning once. If you are using micro-fry, using a serving spoon, scoop a portion of the whitebait batter mixture into the pan. Cook for 2–3 minutes till golden brown on one side then flip the whitebait and cook on the other side until brown and cooked through.

Remove the cooked whitebait or fritters from the pan using a slotted spoon and drain on paper towels to absorb any excess oil, then serve immediately with mayonnaise and lemon wedges for squeezing, or keep warm in a low oven for up to 30 minutes.

Tip: The fritter recipe works for all sorts of seafood – mussels or winkles are two of my favourites – cook in exactly the same way, just replace whitebait with your choice of seafood. Try serving the fritters with a little Seafood Ketchup from the Prawn Dogs recipe on page 148 for a truly delicious dish.

PAN-FRIED SPRATS
WITH AIOLI

PREPARE: **10 MINUTES** COOK: **15 MINUTES** SERVES: **4**

Eating a whole fish is not for everyone but this is the place to start if you're feeling adventurous. A whole sprat is delicious, simply cooked and eaten with a big dollop of garlicky mayonnaise, or to call it its posh name, aioli.

100 g/¾ cup plain/all-purpose flour

salt and freshly ground black pepper

400 g/14 oz. whole sprats (no more than 10-cm/4-in. long)

a small bunch of fresh salad leaves, to serve

AIOLI

150 g/1 stick plus 2 tablespoons butter

100 g/7 tablespoons mayonnaise

2 garlic cloves, peeled and sliced into 3 slices

Put the flour in a wide shallow dish and season generously with salt and pepper. Lay the sprats on the flour, turning once so to coat evenly.

To make the aioli, put the butter in a large frying pan/skillet set over a medium heat. When the butter is foaming, carefully place the garlic in the pan. Cook for 2 minutes until just beginning to brown. Remove the garlic from the pan and crush the garlic into a small bowl. Add the mayonnaise and mix well.

Return the pan you cooked the garlic in to a medium heat and place the flour-coated sprats in the pan. Cook for 2 minutes on either side. Remove the sprats from the pan using a slotted spoon and drain on paper towels.

Serve on a plate dressed with salad leaves and a generous dollop of aioli.

Tip: If the butter starts to get too brown or too hot, reduce the heat, then add a little more butter to the pan which will foam and bring down the heat of the pan immediately.

ANCHOVY & POTATO GRATIN

PREPARE: **30 MINUTES**   COOK: **2 HOURS**   SERVES: **4**

This is a hearty dish that can be prepared ahead of cooking. It uses the strong saltiness of canned anchovies in an unusual way to deliver a hearty, satisfying dish that can be served on its own with a salad, or as an accompaniment to roast lamb or pork. I've written this assuming you have a food processor fitted with a slicing blade or mandoline, if not it's good practice for your knife skills as there is a lot of slicing required here.

150 g/1½ cups spinach

50 g/2 oz. canned anchovies

4 garlic cloves, peeled

6 roasting potatoes, peeled

3 brown onions, peeled

300 ml/1¼ cups double/heavy cream

a 20 x 25-cm/8 x 10-in. casserole dish

Preheat the oven to 160°C (325°F) Gas 3.

Put the spinach and 50 ml/3½ tablespoons of water in a saucepan set over a medium heat. Cover and cook until steam forms, then immediately remove from the heat. The spinach will wilt.

Transfer the spinach and its cooking liquor to a food processor and add the anchovies and garlic, and blend to a purée. Pour into a bowl and set aside.

Using a slicing blade, very thinly slice the potatoes in the food processor but do not rinse the potatoes after they have been sliced as the starch binds the dish together. Very thinly slice the onions in the same way.

Arrange a thin layer of potatoes on the base of the casserole dish. Using a pastry brush or with a spoon, thinly coat the potato layer with the anchovy, garlic and spinach purée. Next, add a very thin layer of onions. Repeat this layering process as many times as possible, finishing with a layer of potato. Ensure there is enough room left at the top of the dish for expansion while cooking (about 1 cm/⅜ in.).

Pour over most of the cream and leave it to settle for 10 minutes, before adding more cream until the top is just covered.

Cover with foil and bake in the preheated oven for 1½ hours. Check the cooking after 1 hour, then at 15 minute intervals – a knife should cut through all the layers easily and if the potato is soft, the gratin is ready.

Remove the foil and place back in the oven, increasing the temperature to 180°C (350°F) Gas 4 for 10 minutes, to brown the top.

Slice and serve the gratin like you would a lasagne.

Tips: If you do not have a slicing blade for the food processor, you could slice the potatoes and onion using a mandoline or with care using a small sharp knife by hand. You can store the gratin in the fridge for up to 4 days once it has been cooked but do not crisp at the higher temperature. To reheat from chilled, bake the gratin at 180°C (350°F) Gas 4 for 25 minutes.

SARDINE CROSTINI

PREPARE: **15 MINUTES** COOK: **15 MINUTES** MAKES: **4**

These crostini can make a lovely light lunch or you can scale down the recipe to make canapés. Salty, grilled sardines work perfectly with the flavour of fresh tomatoes.

4 slices crusty white bread

1 garlic clove, peeled and cut in half

8 whole sardines (each about 100 g/ 3½ oz.), scaled, gutted and heads and tails discarded

2 brown onions, peeled and sliced into rings

4 tomatoes, diced into 5-mm/¼-in. pieces

a small bunch of fresh basil, to serve

salt and freshly ground black pepper, to season

Toast the bread slices under a medium grill/broiler until lightly golden.

Rub the garlic cut-side down on each slice of toasted bread. This will give a hint of garlic to the finished crostinis but it won't overpower the other flavours in the dish.

Preheat a frying pan/skillet over a medium heat. Add the sardines to the dry pan to cook for about 10 minutes, turning the fish every minute or so, until they are cooked through and slightly blackened.

Take the pan off the heat and immediately add the onions. After 30 seconds add the tomatoes. There should be enough residual heat in the pan to heat the tomatoes through but not overcook them.

Place 2 sardines on each slice of toasted bread, cover with a few spoonfuls of tomato and onion mixture. Dress with a few basil leaves and season with salt and pepper before serving.

STARGAZY PIE

PREPARE: **30 MINUTES** COOK: **30 MINUTES** SERVES: **4**

Stargazy pie, also called 'starry gazey pie', is a Cornish dish normally made with pilchards. The unique feature of a stargazy pie is the fish heads that protrude through the pastry crust, so that they appear to be gazing skyward at the stars. This also allows the oils from the fish that are released during cooking flow back into the pie for extra flavour.

2 carrots, peeled and finely diced

2 celery stalks, finely diced

2 brown onions, peeled and finely diced

50 g/3½ tablespoons butter

600 ml/2½ cups Fish Stock (see page 11)

300 g/10 oz. mussels, cleaned

100 ml/7 tablespoons double/heavy cream

20 ml/1½ tablespoons Pernod (or other aniseed-based liqueur)

salt and freshly ground black pepper

a bunch of fresh flat-leaf parsley, finely chopped

150 g/5½ oz. hake, diced

100 g/3½ oz. readymade puff pastry

4 whole sardines (100 g/3½ oz.), scaled, gutted and cut in half

1 egg, beaten

1 quantity Buttered New Potatoes (see page 46), to serve

a 30-cm/12-in. casserole dish

Put the carrots, celery and onions in a large saucepan with the butter set over a low heat. Cook for 10 minutes, then add the fish stock and bring to a simmer. Add the mussels and cook until the mussels begin to open. As soon as the mussels have opened, take the pan off the heat, strain the contents, preserving the liquor. Remove the mussels and shell them, discarding the shells. Set the meat aside.

Pour the liquor back into the saucepan, add the cream and bring to a rolling simmer for about 10 minutes, until the volume of the liquor has reduced by one-third. Stir through the Pernod then transfer the liquor to a jug/pitcher, cover and chill in the fridge.

Preheat the oven to 180°C (350°F) Gas 4.

To assemble the pie, pour the liquor into the casserole dish, seasoning with a pinch of salt and pepper. Sprinkle with parsley and add the hake and reserved mussels.

Roll out the pastry on a lightly floured surface to a thickness of 3 mm/⅛ in. Lift the pastry using the rolling pin and carefully drape over the casserole dish. Trim the edges using the back of a knife and make a pattern around the edges using a fork. Using a sharp knife, slice through the pastry in eight places. Poke the head and tail of each sardine through the openings in the pastry lid. Brush with the beaten egg to form a glaze, taking extra care to seal the pastry around the sardines.

Bake in the preheated oven for 20–25 minutes, until golden brown.

Serve immediately with buttered new potatoes.

ROUND FISH

This chapter takes us around the world for a taste of my favourite cuisines.

The Seafood Gumbo (page 78) is a classic dish from Louisiana with French, Spanish, West African, German and Choctaw influences. Whether it started as a version of bouillabaisse or a West African fish stew is a debate where the true answer is lost to history. I love the blend of flavours in a gumbo and the wonderful mix of food cultures it evokes.

Try cooking the Bouillabaisse (page 74) as an example of classic French Marseilles cuisine. Mine balances the flavours of tomato, aniseed, (bell) peppers and seafood accompanied by garlic and crusty French bread: it brings with it a feeling of Mediterranean warmth and sea aromas every time I eat this brilliant dish.

Haddock with Potato Cakes, Poached Egg & Hollandaise Sauce (page 81) wins the prize for the longest title in the book. It is also, to me, the epitome of a satisfying English brunch. It's truly delicious and perfect for a cold spring morning.

Goan Fish Curry (page 70) is mild and surprisingly easy to cook. Like the bouillabaisse and the gumbo it is an interpretation of the classic dish, a balanced and tasty meal that my family love.

Thai Fishcakes (page 85), Japanese-inspired Roast Cod with Miso & Nori (page 86), Spanish Salt Cod Brandade (page 82) and Salt-baked Sea Bass (page 77) are here too for you to try different techniques and styles of cooking.

GOAN FISH CURRY

PREPARE: **20 MINUTES** COOK: **20 MINUTES** SERVES: **4**

This curry starts with a masala spice blend. I've included my homemade version but there are good readymade blends available in most supermarkets. The key here is the blend of hot spice, sweet coconut and a little sourness to balance the wonderful aromatic and satisfying flavours without overpowering the fish.

2 teaspoons brown sugar

2 teaspoons chilli/hot red pepper flakes

3 garlic cloves

1 tablespoon grated fresh ginger

1 brown onion, peeled and finely chopped

vegetable oil, for frying

140 g/scant ½ cup tomato purée/paste

400 ml/1²/₃ cups canned coconut milk

25 ml/1½ tablespoons white wine vinegar

salt

6 red chillies/chiles, thinly sliced

400 g/14 oz. firm white fish (such as plaice or pollock), chopped into bite-sized pieces

8 large uncooked prawns/shrimp, shells on

½ teaspoon mustard seeds

a small handful of dried curry leaves

boiled rice, to serve

MASALA SPICE BLEND

1 teaspoon whole cloves

1 tablespoon coriander seeds

1 teaspoon cumin seeds

3 black peppercorns

½ teaspoon ground turmeric

½ star anise

Begin by making the masala spice blend. Preheat a frying pan/skillet over a medium heat. Put all of the spices in the dry pan and gently stir until they are strongly aromatic and starting to brown. Take off the heat and, using a pestle and mortar, grind the spices to a fine powder.

Add the sugar, chilli/hot red pepper flakes, garlic, ginger and onion to the ground spices and mash together with the pestle in the mortar.

Pour a little oil in a deep saucepan set over a medium heat. Add the spice mixture with the tomato purée/paste and cook until hot and bubbling. Slowly add the coconut milk and simmer for a couple of minutes – the mixture should be quite wet, like single/light cream; add a little water to thin it out if needed. Stir in the vinegar, taste and season with a little salt.

Add the sliced fresh chilli/chile, then the fish pieces and prawns/shrimp. Cook until the prawns/shrimp are cooked through and pink in colour.

In the pan you used to warm the spices, quickly fry the mustard seeds and curry leaves with a little vegetable oil until the mustard seeds start to pop in the heat. Scatter over the curry and serve with boiled rice.

FISH PIE

PREPARE: **2 HOURS 45 MINUTES** COOK: **20 MINUTES** SERVES: **4-6**

The first rule of fish pie is that there are no rules. My fish pie has a puff pastry top, the king of white fish, cod, bacon lardons and saffron with some added shellfish. As with many of my recipes, you can use this as a starting point for your own pie and improvise with the fish and/or shellfish you have available. This is the pie I want to eat on a cold, dark evening with a group of friends and a few bottles of stout to accompany it.

500 g/18 oz. purged clams

500 g/18 oz. mussels, cleaned and debearded

200 ml/¾ cup white wine

500 ml/2 cups Fish Stock (see page 11)

25 g/1¾ tablespoons butter

100 g/3½ oz. smoked bacon, diced into 1-cm/⅜-in. lardons

2 teaspoons plain/all-purpose flour

a pinch of saffron threads

salt, to season

500 g/18 oz. cod fillet, skinned, boned and diced

500 g/18 oz. readymade puff pastry

1 egg, beaten

TO SERVE (OPTIONAL)

300 g/11 oz. potatoes, peeled, diced and boiled

50 g/3½ tablespoons butter, melted

seasonal vegetables, steamed

First, prepare the clams and mussels. Put them in a large saucepan, with the wine, set over a medium heat and cook until they just open. Remove the clams and mussels and shell them, discarding the shells. Set the meat aside.

Carefully spoon the remaining liquor from the saucepan into the fish stock and stir. There is usually some grit left at the bottom of the saucepan, so be careful to leave that behind – I usually leave some of the liquor to ensure I don't transfer any grit

Put the butter and lardons in a large saucepan set over a medium heat and cook until the lardons are starting to crisp and caramelize.

Carefully spoon the lardons onto a plate and set aside, leaving all the fat in the pan. Reduce the heat, add the flour to the pan and stir into the bacon fat – it should be enough to form a crumbly mixture but add a little more flour if needed.

With the pan on the heat, slowly add the stock mixture, whisking all the time until a thick paste is formed. Continue whisking until the mixture is the consistency of double/heavy cream. Add the saffron and whisk into the sauce. Taste and season with a little salt, ½ teaspoon should be enough.

Add the reserved clams, mussels and bacon with the cod to the sauce and mix together. Pour into a large casserole dish, place a pie form in the centre and set in the fridge to cool for at least 2 hours.

Preheat the oven to 160°C (325°F) Gas 3.

Roll out the pastry on a lightly floured surface to a thickness of 3 mm/⅛ in. Lift the pastry using the rolling pin and carefully drape over the casserole dish. Squeeze off the excess around the sides with your thumb and make gentle indentations with a fork around the edges. Glaze the top with the beaten egg. Using the leftover pastry, make fish shapes to decorate the top.

Bake in the preheated oven for 35 minutes, plus 5–10 minutes if using a deep casserole dish.

Serve with boiled potatoes tossed in melted butter, and seasonal vegetables.

BOUILLABAISSE

PREPARE: **30 MINUTES** COOK: **1 HOUR** SERVES: **4**

The king of all fish dishes, this French Provençal dish is one of my favourite seafood dishes to make. I've included my 'secret' ingredient, a blackened pepper, which adds a sweetness to balance the sharpness of the tomatoes. This dish is not for the faint-hearted as there are bones and shells to pick through, but it is proper finger food, definitely not a dish to wear a white shirt to eat. The name 'bouillabaisse' comes from the phrases 'to boil' and 'to simmer'. The fish should be boiled in salty water, then simmered in a tomato-based stock. Triple the quantities to transform this into a summer feast for ten people – it makes a great talking point and is a magnificent celebration of seafood.

1 baguette, sliced diagonally into 5-mm/¼-in. slices, lightly toasted

4 hake steaks (each about 100 g/3½ oz.)

8 extra-large/colossal prawns/shrimp, shells and heads on

800 g/1¾ lbs. mussels, cleaned

200 g/1½ cups peeled and cooked small new potatoes

50 ml/3½ tablespoons Pernod (or other aniseed-based liqueur)

salt, to season

150 g/5½ oz. smoked or cured salmon (see page 19)

fresh flat-leaf parsley, chopped

SAUCE

1 brown onion, peeled and sliced

2 garlic cloves, peeled and sliced

a pinch of saffron threads

½ fennel bulb, sliced

olive oil

1 red (bell) pepper

300 ml/1¼ cups Fish Stock (see page 11)

1 teaspoon caster/granulated sugar

a small bunch of thyme, sage and bay, tied into a bouquet garni

500 g/18 oz. fish heads (if available)

800 g/4 cups canned chopped tomatoes

ROUILLE

200 ml/¾ cup mayonnaise

2 garlic cloves, peeled and crushed

a small pinch of saffron threads

Begin by making the sauce. Put the onion, garlic, saffron and fennel in a large saucepan with a generous amount of oil (about 5-mm/¼-in. deep) and cook over a low heat for about 5 minutes to brown everything slightly.

Carefully place the (bell) pepper over a naked flame on a gas stovetop to blacken turning once (if you do not have a gas stovetop, place under a grill/broiler on a high heat for 5 minutes). Peel away most of the skin, then slice the flesh and add to the sauce.

Add the fish stock, sugar, bouquet garni, fish heads and tomatoes and bring to a low simmer for 45 minutes.

Remove the fish heads and bouquet garni then, purée using a handheld electric blender to a smooth liquid. Store the sauce in the fridge or freezer – it actually improves if stored for a day in the fridge.

Next make the rouille by mixing the mayonnaise, garlic and saffron together in a large mixing bowl using a handheld electric blender. Set aside until ready to serve.

Toast the bread slices under a medium grill/broiler until lightly golden. Set aside until ready to serve.

For the bouillabaise, bring a pan of heavily salted water to a simmer and add the hake. Cook for 4 minutes until opaque and just starting to break up.

Lift the hake from the water and put in a large saucepan with the prawns, mussels, potatoes and chilled sauce. Set over a medium heat and bring to a low simmer for 5 minutes. Add the Pernod and stir gently, then taste and season with salt, if needed.

Pour the bouillabaisse into deep bowls, arranging the fish and shellfish for presentation. Top each with cured salmon and sprinkle with chopped parsley. Serve with the rouille, baguette slices and a side plate for bones and shells.

SALT-BAKED SEA BASS

PREPARE: **50 MINUTES** COOK: **45 MINUTES** SERVES: **4**

This method of cooking poaches the fish in its own juices and introduces a mild saltiness to the sea bass. The pastry will break off dramatically when serving and should take the skin off with it, leaving perfectly cooked sea bass. Try this with any large round fish that is in season or that is available to you and serve with roasted vegetables or a Summer-fresh salad and buttered new potatoes.

200 g/1 cup sea salt

5 eggs, plus 1 egg, beaten

700 g/5²/₃ cups plain/all-purpose flour

1 large whole sea bass (800 g–1 kg/ 28–35 oz.), scaled and gutted

a small bunch of fresh flat-leaf parsley, chopped, plus extra to garnish

1 lemon, cut into quarters

TO SERVE

800 g/6 cups new potatoes, boiled

30 g/2 tablespoons butter, melted

400 g/3 cups trimmed green beans

Preheat the oven to 150°C (300°F) Gas 2.

Mix together the salt, 5 eggs and 650 g/scant 5 cups of the flour in a large mixing bowl with enough water to make a firm but pliable dough. Set in the fridge to rest for at least 30 minutes. Roll out on a lightly floured surface to a thickness of about 6 mm/¼ in.

Stuff the bass with the chopped parsley and lemon wedges, then roll up in the dough. Seal tightly by crimping the pastry with your fingers around the fish. Glaze with the beaten egg.

Bake in the preheated oven for 45 minutes. Remove and rest for 5 minutes before serving on a large platter dressed with parsley leaves.

Serve with boiled new potatoes, drenched in melted butter and blanched green beans.

SEAFOOD GUMBO

PREPARE: **30 MINUTES** COOK: **1 HOUR** SERVES: **4**

Gumbo is the state dish of Louisiana and so comes with much history and pride. The dish is a fusion of French, Spanish, African and Native American cuisines, a reflection of this wonderful state's culture. There are many ways to cook gumbo. Start with my recipe, but do experiment with the spicing and heat to make it your own. I add chorizo to give it a smoky depth of flavour but you can leave this out for a lighter version. You can use the same base recipe with chicken rather than fish stock for a meat gumbo. The key flavour comes from making a roux from oil and flour, okra/ladies fingers and the 'Holy Trinity' of onion, celery and green (bell) pepper. Okra/ladies fingers can be tricky to find but many supermarkets or Asian supermarkets now stock it.

150 ml/²⁄₃ cup vegetable oil

100 g/³⁄₄ cup plain/all-purpose flour

200 g/3⅓ cups chopped okra/ladies fingers, finely chopped

2 brown onions, peeled and finely chopped

2 celery stalks, finely chopped

2 green (bell) peppers, finely chopped

150 g/1¼ cups sliced cooking chorizo

1 litre/1³⁄₄ pints Fish Stock (see page 11)

1 teaspoon cayenne pepper

400 g/2 cups canned chopped tomatoes

a dash of Tabasco

salt, to season

200 g/7 oz. white fish fillet (such as whiting, pollack or hake), diced

8 uncooked large prawns/shrimp

boiled rice, to serve (optional)

a small bunch of fresh flat-leaf parsley, chopped

Make a roux by mixing 120 ml/½ cup of the oil with the flour in a saucepan set over a low heat. Bring the temperature up slowly, stirring continuously, until the mixture has a colour similat to a cup of milky tea – with practice you may want to make this darker for a deeper flavour. Once the colour is achieved take off the heat and keep stirring for a couple of minutes until the roux has cooled down.

In a separate pan, sweat the chopped vegetables and chorizo over a medium heat for a couple of minutes then slowly add the roux while stirring. Once combined and hot, add the stock by pouring it into the mixture while still stirring. Add the cayenne pepper and canned tomatoes and stir well.

Simmer this mixture for 45 minutes to allow the flavours to infuse.

Leave the mixture as it is or blend using a handheld electric blender to make a smooth, thick sauce. I prefer it unblended but if serving with rice it is better when blended.

Add the Tabasco to give a bit more heat, then season with salt to taste.

The sauce now can be kept in the fridge or frozen and the seafood added fresh when you are ready to serve.

Finally, the seafood: add the fish and prawns/shrimp to the sauce and simmer until the prawns/shrimp have cooked and are pink in colour. Remove from the heat and serve straight away on its own or with boiled rice. Dress with chopped parsley and enjoy.

HADDOCK WITH POTATO CAKES, POACHED EGG & HOLLANDAISE SAUCE

PREPARE: **10 MINUTES** COOK: **30 MINUTES** SERVES: **4**

It doesn't get much more comforting than this: a delicious fillet of haddock, an oozy poached egg with hollandaise and some fried mashed potato cakes to mop it all up with – this is heaven on a plate for me.

600 g/3 cups Mash (see page 105)

butter, for frying

1 teaspoon white wine vinegar

4 eggs

4 x 150 g/5½ oz. haddock fillets, skinned and boned

a small bunch of fresh garlic chives, thinly sliced

salt and freshly ground black pepper

HOLLANDAISE SAUCE

250 g/2 sticks plus 1 tablespoon butter

4 egg yolks

salt

freshly squeezed juice of ½ lemon

a 500-ml/18-oz. capacity jug/pitcher

Cook the mashed potatoes following the method on page 105. Set a large frying pan/skillet over a high heat and add a little butter – it should colour and caramelize a little as you cook. Make 4 patties with the mashed potatoes and put them in the warm pan to cook for 2 minutes on either side. Keep warm in a low oven until ready to serve.

Make the hollandaise just before you start cooking the fish and eggs so it is still hot. Heat the butter in a saucepan set over a low heat until just melted, then leave to cool for a few minutes. Add the yolks, a pinch of salt and the lemon juice to the jug/pitcher and whisk on high with a handheld electric blender. Slowly pour the hot butter, while still whisking, into the jug/pitcher to form a pale yellow sauce.

Bring a large pan of water (about 5-cm/2-in. deep) to the boil over a high heat, add the vinegar and turn off the heat. Break the eggs into the water one at a time and leave to cook in the warm water for 6–8 minutes – you might need to heat the water a little to finish cooking.

Put a knob of butter in a large non-stick frying pan/skillet set over a medium heat until the base is covered and the butter is just starting to foam. Season with salt and place the haddock fillets in the pan. Cook until they are opaque two-thirds of the way through, then finish cooking by spooning over the hot butter – they should be caramelized and brown on the bottom and pale, but cooked on the top.

Serve on large hot plates. Place a warm potato cake on each plate, then a haddock fillet, crispy-side up, a poached egg and lashings of hollandaise sauce. Sprinkle with chives to finish and enjoy.

SALT COD BRANDADE

PREPARE: **24 HOURS 20 MINUTES** COOK: **30 MINUTES** SERVES: **8–10**

A wonderful French Mediterranean dish, this can be a simple lunch on its own, served as an appetizer before a larger meal, or even as part of a banquet of smaller dishes. Brandade can be made without the potatoes for a cleaner flavour but I prefer the creaminess that the potatoes add to the dish.

500 g/18 oz. cod fillet, skinned and boned

salt, to season

1 brown onion, peeled and diced

4 garlic cloves, peeled and thinly sliced

200 g/½ lb. Maris Piper potatoes, peeled and diced

200 ml/¾ cup whole milk

100 ml/⅓ cup olive oil, plus extra for drizzling

100 ml/⅓ cup double/heavy cream

1 baguette, sliced diagonally into 5-mm/¼-in. slices

SALAD, TO SERVE

1 cucumber, peeled and finely diced

a small bunch of fresh dill, thinly sliced

1 small fennel bulb, thinly sliced

grated zest and freshly squeezed juice of 1 lemon

Begin by making the salad. Toss the cucumber, dill, fennel and lemon zest and juice together in a large mixing bowl. Set aside for at least 1 hour in advance so the flavours can combine and to mute the fennel slightly.

Generously season the cod fillet with salt on both sides and set in the fridge for at least 24 hours.

Rinse and pat dry, then put the cod fillet, onion, garlic, potatoes and milk in a saucepan set over a gentle heat. Bring to a low simmer for 20 minutes, check the potatoes are fully cooked then strain off any excess milk.

While still hot, transfer the mixture to a food processor and blend. With the motor running, slowly pour in the oil and double/heavy cream. You should now have a thick paste.

Toast the bread slices under a medium grill/broiler until lightly golden.

Serve the branade, drizzled with oil and sprinkled with black pepper, alongside the salad and toasts.

THAI FISHCAKES

PREPARE: **15 MINUTES** COOK: **10 MINUTES** SERVES: **4**

One of my favourite dishes, this always transports me back to a beach in Thailand, where I was lucky enough to live for a short while. No potatoes or egg are used in these fishcakes and the resulting tough but tasty skin formed upon cooking is delicious.

3 garlic cloves, peeled

1 red chilli/chile

2 brown onions, peeled and chopped

1 teaspoon chilli powder

½ teaspoon ground cumin

½ teaspoon ground coriander

50 g/5 tablespoons grated fresh ginger

1 teaspoon tamarind paste

grated zest and freshly squeezed juice of 1 lime

2 tablespoons fish sauce

400 g/14 oz. white fish fillet (such as hake, pollock, whiting or cod), chopped into 2-cm/¾-in. pieces

vegetable oil, for frying

DIPPING SAUCE

2 tablespoons brown sugar

1 tablespoon dark soy sauce

2 tablespoons sesame oil

1 tablespoon fish sauce

freshly squeezed juice of 1 lime

½ carrot, finely diced

½ cucumber, finely diced

Begin by making the dipping sauce. Heat the sugar, soy sauce, sesame oil and fish sauce in a saucepan set over a medium heat. Remove from the heat and let cool, before adding the lime juice, carrot and cucumber. Set aside until ready to serve.

Put the garlic, chilli/chile and onions in a food processor and pulse until finely chopped and combined. Add the spices, ginger, tamarind, lime zest and juice and fish sauce, and pulse again to combine. Finally, add the fish pieces and pulse briefly until fully combined – it should be the texture of a thick porridge. Don't over-blend the mixture once the fish has been added as it can easily become a paste.

Heat a little vegetable oil in a saucepan set over a medium heat. Scoop tablespoonfuls of the mixture into the hot pan. After about a minute, flip the fishcakes over and cook for a further minute, until golden brown.

Serve warm with the dipping sauce.

ROAST COD WITH MISO & NORI

PREPARE: **10 MINUTES** COOK: **30 MINUTES** SERVES: **4**

Cod is the classic fish-and-chips fish but it really is so much more than that. With farmed and line-caught fish now available there are sustainable stocks to be found. This recipe suits a centrepiece platter for a sharing meal but by reducing the cooking times you can also make individual portions using fillet. The miso and nori add the savoury and salt flavours that offset the sweetness of cod and the richness of the pak choi/bok choy that it is served on.

1 whole cod or pollock (about 1.2 kg/2½ lbs.)

vegetable oil

sea salt flakes

50 g/3½ tablespoons pale miso paste

50 ml/3½ tablespoons light soy sauce

4 nori sheets

2 pak choi/bok choy, halved and steamed

100 g/1 cup cooked dried rice noodles

4 red chillies/chiles, thinly sliced

a large baking sheet, lined with a silicone mat

Preheat the oven to 160°C (325°F) Gas 3.

Trim the cod of its dorsal and pectoral fins with a pair of scissors, ensure the cavity has been properly cleaned including the bloodline on the backbone and that the fish is scaled.

Oil the cod and add a sprinkle of sea salt to the cavity. Place on the baking sheet and bake in the preheated oven for 20–25 minutes until the temperature on the backbone is 50°C (120°F) when tested with a meat thermometer.

Take the fish out of the oven and turn the heat up to 200°C (400°F) Gas 6.

Remove the skin from the body of the fish – it should peel away easily.

Mix miso and soy together to make a paste and brush over the fish meat. Now wrap the fish with the nori sheets. Return the fish to the baking sheet and bake again in the oven for 5 minutes.

Serve the cod whole on a platter with steamed pak choi/bok choy, cooked rice noodles and chillies/chiles. Cut and portion the fish at the table for an exciting and tasty feast.

Tip: To cook this dish using cod or pollock fillets, preheat the oven to 200°C (400°F) Gas 6, then pan fry the descaled fillets in a hot pan for 5 minutes skin-side down, until the skin is brown and crispy and the meat is opaque about two-thirds of the way through. Brush the top of the fillet with the miso and soy mixture and cover with nori. Place in the oven for 5 minutes to finish then serve as above.

GURNARD WITH OVEN-ROASTED TOMATOES

PREPARE: **10 MINUTES**   COOK: **20 MINUTES**   SERVES: **4**

This dish is all about drama. Serving a whole fish on a plate has a lot of impact, particularly when the fish is unusual, like a gurnard. Gurnards have a strong flavour and balance the robust flavour of roasted tomatoes well.

4 whole gurnard (each about 400 g/ 14 oz.), gutted, cleaned and scaled

plain/all-purpose flour

salt, to season

vegetable oil, to drizzle

2 brown onions, peeled and roughly chopped

2 lemons, quartered

a small bunch of fresh lemon thyme

16–24 vine tomatoes

balsamic vinegar, to season

TO SERVE (OPTIONAL)

300 g/11 oz. potatoes, peeled and diced

50 g/3½ tablespoons butter, melted

a small bunch of fresh flat-leaf parsley, chopped

Preheat the oven to 180°C (350°F) Gas 4.

Carefully trim the gurnards with a pair of scissors to remove all their fins and sharp spikes.

Spoon some flour onto a plate and lightly season it with salt. Roll the gurnard in the flour, then drizzle a little oil over them and gently rub it over the fish.

In each belly cavity, place ½ onion, 2 lemon wedges and a couple of sprigs of lemon thyme. Place the gurnard on a baking sheet and bake in the preheated oven for 20 minutes.

Put the tomatoes on a separate baking sheet, lightly drizzle with oil and season with salt and a splash of balsamic vinegar. Add to the oven 5 minutes after the fish goes in.

Check the fish is cooked using a meat thermometer – the meat should be at a temperature of at least 58°C (136°F) but no more than 65°C (150°F).

Serve the gunard whole on a plate with the roasted tomatoes and some cooked new potatoes tossed in butter and parsley. Decorate with lemon thyme sprinkled over the top.

FLAT FISH

Flat fish are my staple fish for the restaurants: dramatic served whole, easy to fillet, quick to cook and delicious to eat, what more does a chef want?

When scuba diving, a very sharp eye is needed to spot these camouflage experts as they lie on the sea bottom in wait for their dinner. They remain still, trusting in their camouflage over escape, but when they do swim they are fast and seem to fly across the sea floor before disappearing again into the sea bed.

The fish in this chapter range from the stunning, plate-sized Dover sole to the huge deep sea halibut, each has its own characteristics and the recipes are designed to match the fish but do mix and match any of the recipes using whichever fish you can buy.

Serving fish whole gives great impact and is seen regularly on my menus. Don't be afraid of making the sauces that accompany them, they are surprisingly easy to do.

I've included a filleting guide on page 97 but I do recommend you have the fishmonger prepare it for you. Always ask to keep the bones as flat fish make some of the best stocks. If you do want to prepare them yourself then ask your fishmonger to show you how and practise on cheaper varieties at first. Some flat fish are very expensive, a good Dover sole will cost a similar price to fillet steak but this doesn't mean they aren't worth the expense. In the United Kingdom, plaice and dabs are well priced when they are in season. It seems obvious but buy fresh, in-season varieties – they taste best and will be well priced.

DOVER SOLE MEUNIÈRE

PREPARE: **10 MINUTES** COOK: **10 MINUTES** SERVES: **4**

If there is a classic recipe for Dover sole it's this. A meunière sauce is a brown butter and lemon sauce that provides a delicious balance to the wonderful flavour of Dover sole. The sole is lightly dredged in flour before cooking, which is where the name meunière comes from, the literal translation being 'miller's wife'. This recipe requires a delicate touch when cooking so as to not overcook the fish. Ask your fishmonger to skin the sole – the skin is so tough and coarse it was once used as sandpaper, not something you want to eat!

plain/all-purpose flour

salt, to season

4 whole Dover sole (each about 500 g/ 18 oz.), skinned

vegetable oil

250 g/2 sticks plus 1 tablespoon butter

freshly squeezed juice of 2 lemons

a small bunch of fresh flat-leaf parsley, finely chopped

2 large baking sheets, greased and lined with baking parchment

Preheat the oven to 200°C (400°F) Gas 6.

Cover a large plate with flour and season with a little salt.

Drag the sole in the flour to lightly coat then arrange on the prepared baking sheets. Drizzle with oil and rub all over to coat the fish.

Bake the fish in the preheated oven for 10 minutes to cook and test that the fish is cooked by inserting a toothpick at the thickest part of the fish – if the flesh is soft, the fish is cooked, if it is still tough then return to the oven for another couple of minutes and check again.

Meanwhile, make the sauce by melting the butter in a saucepan set over a medium heat – the butter will foam when it has melted as the water in the butter boils. As soon as the foaming has stopped the butter will start to cook. We want the butter to cook a little, until a distinctive nutty, hazelnut aroma is given off. Remove from the heat the moment this is achieved. Allow the butter to cool a little, then add the lemon juice and gently whisk together.

Reheat the sauce if necessary but do not let it boil.

Serve the fish whole, cover generously with the sauce and a sprinkle of chopped parsley.

LEMON SOLE WITH SHRIMP & CAPER SAUCE ON A BED OF BAKED LEEKS

PREPARE: **10 MINUTES** COOK: **1½ HOURS** SERVES: **2**

Lemon sole has a delicate and delicious flavour. This recipe balances the sole with Mediterranean hints from wonderful salty capers and marjoram, while the addition of shrimps and leeks makes for a satisfying and sumptuous meal.

2 leeks, sliced into 1-cm/⅜-in. rounds

100 g/7 tablespoons butter, diced, plus extra for frying

a small bunch of fresh marjoram

1 teaspoon Dijon mustard

salt and freshly ground black pepper

2 whole lemon sole (each about 600 g/ 21 oz.), filleted

200 g/½ cup brown shrimps

100 g/½ cup capers

Preheat the oven to 140°C (275°F) Gas 1.

Spread the sliced leeks on a baking sheet and cover with the diced butter, marjoram sprigs and mustard, and season with a pinch of salt. Cover with foil and bake in the preheated oven for 1½ hours.

Heat a little butter in a large frying pan/skillet set over a medium heat, until just foaming. Lightly sprinkle salt on the lemon sole fillets, then carefully place them skin-side down in the pan (place them in the pan away from you so that the oil doesn't splash and burn you). Apply a little pressure initially using the flat blade of a fish slice to stop them curling up. Once all the fillets are in the pan, turn the heat down and continue cooking until the meat has become two-thirds opaque. Add the shrimps and capers and cover. Continue to cook for another minute until the fillets are cooked through – they should be crisp on the skin-side and just cooked through on top.

To serve, place a generous portion of the baked leeks on a plate, place the fillets on top and dress with the shrimps and caper and some of the sauce from the pan.

Tip: Store the fish bones left over from the whole lemon sole in a sealable bag in the freezer and use them for making stock at another time (see page 11).

PLAICE FISH FINGERS WITH TARTARE SAUCE

PREPARE **10 MINUTES** COOK **15 MINUTES** SERVES: **4**

I love a good fish finger/stick and these are some of the best, they're not perfectly rectangular but then again, neither are fish. These goujons have lots of flavour and plaice make the ideal base.

2 slices of white bread

salt, to season

1 heaped teaspoon smoked paprika

30 g/½ cup grated fresh Parmesan cheese

plain/all-purpose flour

1 egg, gently beaten

vegetable oil, for frying

2 whole plaice (each about 225 g/8 oz.), skinned, filleted and sliced into finger-sized portions

TARTARE SAUCE

100 ml/7 tablespoons mayonnaise

½ red onion, peeled and finely diced

1 teaspoon Dijon mustard

15 g/1½ tablespoons capers

15 g/1½ tablespoons cornichons, thinly sliced

Preheat the oven to 180°C (350°F) Gas 4.

Make the tartare sauce by mixing all of the ingredients together. Set aside.

Put the bread slices directly onto the shelf of the preheated oven and bake for 5 minutes, until it is crispy and golden. Cool then place in a resealable bag. Crush to coarse breadcrumbs using a rolling pin, add a generous pinch of salt, the paprika and Parmesan, reseal the bag and shake to combine. Transfer to a large plate, and on separate plates, put the flour and beaten egg.

Heat a little oil (about 2-mm/⅟₁₆-in. deep) in a large frying pan/skillet set over a medium heat. Drag the plaice portions through the flour, then the egg and finally the breadcrumbs before carefully placing in the pan. Cook on each side for 1 minute, until golden brown, then serve immediately with the tartare sauce.

HOW TO FILLET FLAT FISH

1 Hold the fish using a kitchen cloth (if preferred) and cut around the back of the head to the backbone.

2 Similarly, cut across the tail.

3 Using the tip of the knife against the central backbone, slide the fillet knife under the fillet and slice it away from the frame. Fold the fillet over the backbone carefully removing it.

4 Cut the remaining fillet away from the bones and check for any bone fragments using your fingertips and remove them with fish tweezers.

PARSLEY & PLAICE PUFF PASTRY PIE

PREPARE: **40 MINUTES** COOK: **1 HOUR 10 MINUTES**
SERVES: **4**

A puff pastry fish pie is perfect as a family or a dinner party meal. The parsley and bacon just add layers of flavour to the sauce and the result is a pie I guarantee you'll make time and again.

Put the bacon, onion and garlic in a large saucepan with a little butter (or use all of the butter if you decide not to use bacon in this recipe). Fry over a gentle heat until the onion and garlic are translucent and the bacon is cooked and just starting to brown. Add the fish stock and bring to a rolling simmer. Continue to simmer until the stock has reduced by half.

Add the potatoes and simmer 5 minutes, then add the cream, cheese and parsley and continue to simmer for another 5 minutes. Stir and taste. Add a pinch of salt, if needed, and the white pepper.

8 rashers/strips smoked streaky/fatty bacon (optional), sliced into squares

1 brown onion, peeled and diced

2 garlic cloves, peeled and thinly sliced

50 g/3½ tablespoons butter

1 litre/1¾ pints Fish Stock (see page 11)

3 medium potatoes, peeled and diced into 5-mm/¼-in. cubes

100 ml/½ cup double/heavy cream

50 g/½ cup grated Gruyère cheese

a large bunch of fresh flat-leaf parsley, finely chopped

salt

1 teaspoon ground white pepper

1 teaspoon cornflour/cornstarch

600 g/21 oz. plaice fillet, skinned, boned and roughly chopped

350 g/13 oz. readymade puff pastry

1 egg, beaten

a deep 30-cm/12-in. round casserole dish
baking beans

Mix the cornflour/cornstarch with a spoonful or two of the sauce, then add this back to the sauce and stir through to thicken it.

Allow the sauce to cool completely, then add the plaice and set in the fridge.

Preheat the oven to 180°C (350°F) Gas 4.

Roll out 200 g/7 oz. of the pastry on a lightly floured surface to a thickness of about 3 mm/⅛ in. and cover the bottom and sides of the casserole dish. Prick the base of the pastry all over with a fork to allow steam to escape and stop it from puffing up too much. Cover the base with foil and fill with baking beans, then bake in the preheated oven for 10 minutes. Remove from the oven, take out the beads and the foil, then glaze with beaten egg and bake for a second time, for 2 minutes, to seal the pastry. Reduce the heat of the oven to 160°C (325°F) Gas 3.

Roll out the remaining pastry on a lightly floured surface to a thickness of about 3 mm/⅛ in.

Fill the pie base with the chilled pie mixture, then cover with the pastry. Using the leftover pastry, make fish and seafood shapes to decorate the top. Glaze with beaten egg and bake in the oven for 40 minutes.

Serve while hot with salad or new potatoes, if desired.

BRILL PHO

PREPARE: **20 MINUTES**   COOK: **1 HOUR 10 MINUTES**   SERVES: **4**

Pho is a Vietnamese version of a traditional French consommé-based soup. Brill is the perfect fish for this dish because it is a wonderfully mild-flavoured, yet firm fish, so it will hold together and enable the consommé to remain clear.

1 kg/35 oz. whole brill

2 carrots, peeled and chopped

1 brown onion, peeled and chopped

2 celery stalks, chopped

2 garlic cloves, peeled and thinly sliced

2 shallots, peeled and thinly sliced

20 ml/1½ tablespoons sesame oil

a small bunch of fresh coriander/cilantro, finely chopped, leaves reserved to garnish

1 teaspoon fish sauce (Nam Pla)

6 spring onions/scallions, thinly sliced

freshly squeezed juice of 1 lime, plus 1 lime, cut into wedges

Fillet and skin the brill following the instructions on page 97. Use the bones, skin, carrots, onion and celery to make 1 litre/1¾ pints of clear fish stock following the method on page 11.

Put the garlic and shallots with the sesame oil in a large saucepan set over a gentle heat. Add the brill fillets and fry with just enough heat to cook but not to caramelize. Add 2 teaspoons of the chopped coriander/cilantro.

Pour the stock into the pan and bring to a gentle simmer. Add a little fish sauce to season, then add the spring onions/scallions.

Pour in the lime juice and divide the pho between serving bowls. Garnish with coriander/cilantro leaves and a wedge of lime.

Tip: One of my favourite variations of this recipe is to use fresh prawns/shrimp and/or scallops when they are in season. The light saltiness of the prawns/shrimp and scallop meat balances well with the delicate Vietnamese flavours and the prawn/shrimp heads and scallop frills make the most wonderful stock.

TURBOT FILLET WITH ORANGE & FENNEL

PREPARE: **20 MINUTES** COOK: **90 MINUTES** SERVES: **4**

This flavourful meal is surprisingly light and aromatic. Fennel and orange are a delicious flavour combination and by slow cooking the fennel, it becomes tender, much milder and completely irresistible.

4 medium oranges

2 whole fennel bulbs, thinly sliced

150 ml/²⁄₃ cup white wine

20 ml/1½ tablespoons Pernod (or other aniseed-based liqueur)

600 g/21 oz. turbot, skinned, boned and cut into 4 fillets

salt

butter

a handful of fennel fronds

Preheat the oven to 140°C (275°F) Gas 1.

Zest the oranges and juice 2 of them. Peel the other 2 using a sharp knife, discarding the peel and pith. Cut these oranges into segments ensuring no pith is still attached.

Arrange the sliced fennel, half of the orange zest, the orange juice and orange segments in a baking dish with the wine and Pernod. Mix together, cover with foil and bake in the preheated oven for 1½ hours.

Lightly sprinkle the turbot fillets with salt.

When nearly ready to serve, heat enough butter to cover the bottom of a large frying pan/skillet over a medium heat, just foaming. Carefully place the turbot in the pan and cook until the fillet is cooked to two-thirds of the way up. Cover and immediately take off the heat, leave for 5 minutes to rest and finish cooking.

Spoon the baked fennel and orange into serving bowls, then place a turbot fillet on top. Sprinkle with a little of the remaining orange zest and fennel fronds before serving.

HALIBUT STEAK WITH CIDER CREAM SAUCE, CRACKLING & MASH

PREPARE: **20 MINUTES** COOK: **45 MINUTES** SERVES: **4**

This recipe has been a crowd pleaser in my restaurants since we first opened, the combination of the sharpness of cider and the meatiness of a halibut steak work together perfectly. I add a creamy mash and a stick of perfect pork crackling to balance the textures and to add a hit of saltiness, too. This recipe is not for the diet conscious, with its high levels of fat and salt, but is one to be savoured on a special occasion and enjoyed for all its indulgence.

4 strips pork belly skin (ask your butcher for 1-cm/³⁄₈-in. wide x 30-cm/12-in. long), rinsed

4 halibut steaks (each about 150 g/5 oz.)

50 g/3½ tablespoons butter

salt, to season

CIDER CREAM SAUCE

200 ml/¾ cup dry cider

100 ml/⅓ cup sweet apple juice

50 ml/3½ tablespoons double/heavy cream

MASH

1 kg/35 oz. Maris Piper potatoes

150 g/1 stick plus 2 tablespoons butter

100 ml/⅓ cup double/heavy cream

Preheat the oven to 140°C (275°F) Gas 1.

First, prepare the perfect crackling. Place a wire rack over a baking sheet then lay the strips of pork belly skin over the rack – the sheet is to catch the fat and any excess salt. Cover generously with salt to form a layer of salt crystals (most of the salt will fall off while cooking) and cook in the preheated oven for 45 minutes. Check that the crackling is crispy and continue cooking if not fully hardened (you should expect the skin to curl and bend as it cooks).

For the cider cream, pour the cider and apple juice into a saucepan and bring to a simmer over a gentle heat. Simmer for about 15 minutes to burn off the alcohol and reduce the volume by a third. Add the cream and a small pinch of salt to finish.

Next, prepare the mash. Boil the peeled and diced potatoes in a pan of unsalted boiling water until they just start to crumble. Drain off the water and leave to dry in the colander for 10 minutes. Mash the dried potatoes to a smooth consistency (I strongly recommend buying a potato ricer if you like mashed potatoes to achieve a velvet-like mash every time). In a large saucepan, gently melt the butter and cream together, then add the mashed potatoes and heat, stirring with a wooden spoon to combine. When the mash is ready it will pull away from the side of the saucepan when stirred. Season the mash generously, it will take about 1 teaspoon of salt to bring out the flavour but add this in stages and taste as you go so as not to over season.

When the crackling is nearly done, season the halibut steaks with a little salt, then heat the butter in a large frying pan/skillet over a medium heat, until just foaming. Carefully place the halibut in the pan and cook for 2 minutes on each side. Transfer to a baking sheet and bake in the preheated oven for no more than 5 minutes to finish. The meat is cooked perfectly when a toothpick can be pushed through the thickest part without resistance.

Put a generous portion of mash on 4 serving plates and place the halibut steaks on top. Pour over some cider cream sauce and place a stick of crackling on top to finish.

EXOTIC FISH

Monkfish is the common name for an angler fish, an extraordinarily ugly fish that uses a lure to entice their prey into their huge mouths. Due to their strange appearance and enormous bony head, you will usually only see monkfish tails for sale. It is so delicious, however, and often used in curries due to its firm meaty texture. I've used a little harissa to spice it with and made a tasty kebab.

Skate is soft and flavourful, and to be treated with care. Keep the bones as they make the most fantastic stocks. True skate is unlikely to be what you buy from a fishmonger, instead it will be a ray which has a similar taste and is what is called 'skate' by most fishmongers. True skate should be avoided as their stocks are depleted due to overfishing.

Red mullet and snapper are stunning to look at and should be cooked simply like the stuffed Red Mullet with Seaweed (page 115). The red mullet in the United Kingdom Is technically a tropical goatfish that has migrated here as British waters have warmed up.

John Dory is fascinating to look at and delicious to eat, usually only found as a result of by-catch rather than targeted fishing, these will most likely be found on a fishmonger's slab, not in a supermarket.

I used to spear fish for flounder with spotlights among mangrove swamps in New Zealand. They were challenging to catch but made a rewarding meal. The name flounder is used for various species across the world and the recipe for Flounder Fillets with Tarragon Sauce (page 116) can be made using most flat fish. If you're lucky enough to have an abundance of them then try other recipes from the Flat Fish chapter.

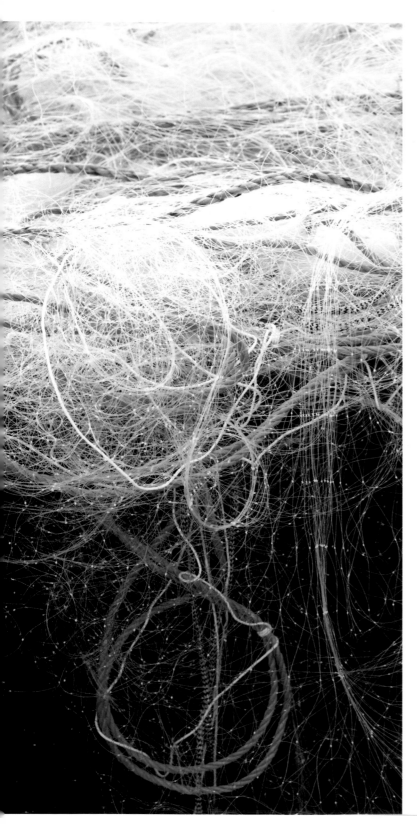

MONKFISH HARISSA KEBABS

PREPARE: **15 MINUTES** COOK: **15 MINUTES** SERVES: **4**

A bit of fun and a taste of the southern Mediterranean. Harissa has chilli/chile, tomato and lemon flavours and these are reflected in these delightful kebabs/kabobs. Monkfish is a firm fish, ideally suited to stronger flavours.

50 g/3½ tablespoons harissa paste

olive oil

600 g/21 oz. monkfish fillet, diced into 2-cm/¾-in. pieces

8 red tomatoes, wedged

2 green (bell) peppers, diced into 2-cm/¾-in. pieces

1 preserved lemon

150 ml/⅔ cup Vegetable Stock (see page 11)

½ teaspoon ground cumin

½ teaspoon ground coriander seeds

½ teaspoon mild chilli powder

100 g/⅔ cup couscous

a small bunch of fresh coriander/cilantro, finely chopped

8 wooden skewers, soaked for 30 minutes

Mix the harissa with a little oil until the mixture is loose and just liquid. Pat the monkfish with paper towels to ensure it is completely dry, then roll it in the harissa mixture to coat thoroughly.

Build the skewers with the monkfish, alternating pieces of tomato and (bell) pepper.

Peel the preserved lemon, reserving the peel. Carefully slice each segment ensuring there is no pith and set aside. Slice the peel into fine matchsticks and set aside.

Bring the stock to a simmer over a gentle heat, add the spices and a little oil, then the couscous. Stir the couscous to remove any lumps then cover and take off the heat, leaving it for 10 minutes to absorb the stock. Once the stock is fully absorbed, fluff the couscous with a fork and add a few pieces of reserved lemon peel to taste.

Set the skewers on a hot stovetop grill pan or a hot barbecue and cook, turning every minute or so until the pepper just starts to blacken. Serve on a bed of couscous and decorate with coriander/cilantro and lemon pieces.

POACHED SKATE WITH CAPERS & CLAMS

PREPARE: **15 MINUTES**   COOK: **10 MINUTES**   SERVES: **4**

As with all good seafood dishes, less is more when it comes to cooking skate. The thickness of skate varies a lot from one side to another so cook it at a lower temperature to ensure it is cooked through without overcooking. Buy your skate skinned and portioned as this is very difficult to do at home. Check your skate and trim off any obvious sinew on the outside of the wing or it will curl while cooking. A trick to ensuring your clams are tender to eat is to freeze them before cooking as it tenderizes the flesh within the shell.

50 g/3½ tablespoons butter

2 skate or ray wings, skinned and divided in 2

1 litre/1¾ pints whole milk

100 g/10 tablespoons capers in saline/brine

400 g/14 oz. surf clams

TO SERVE (OPTIONAL)

300 g/11 oz. potatoes, peeled and diced

50 g/3½ tablespoons butter

a small bunch of fresh flat-leaf parsley, chopped

Put the butter in a large, deep saucepan set over a medium heat and heat till the butter is sizzling. Carefully place the skate in the pan, thick-side down, and cook for a couple of minutes to just caramelize.

Pour over the milk so that it just covers the skate. Add the capers and a few tablespoons of the saline sauce they are in. Add the surf clams and cook until the milk is just starting to form bubbles around the sides of the pan. Remove from the heat and let it sit for 5 minutes, ensuring the clams are cooked and open. The cooking sauce should be about 80°C (175°F) when tested with a sugar thermometer. Return to the heat, if the clams are not cooking, but avoid boiling the milk as it will curdle.

Serve the skate dressed with clams and capers with some sauce spooned over, taking care not to disturb any grit from the clams at the bottom of the pan.

SKATE WITH BEURRE NOISETTE

PREPARE: **15 MINUTES** COOK: **20 MINUTES** SERVES: **2**

As a kid fishing I used to throw rays back as a nuisance fish or use them for cat food. If only I knew then how amazing they would taste! This dish features highly on my meals to eat before I die, it is just so simple, so full of flavour and just perfection on a plate. I've written the recipe giving a whole wing per serving – you could halve the wing and add a side of potatoes or vegetables but I always want a whole wing to myself. The skill of this dish is in making the butter sauce: achieving the hazelnut aroma and flavour and stopping it from overcooking and becoming acrid.

plain/all-purpose flour

salt

2 medium skate or ray wings (each about 500–600 g/18–21 oz.)

vegetable oil

250 g/2 sticks plus 1 tablespoon butter

1 lemon, cut into wedges

sea salt

2 large baking sheets, lined with silicone mats

Preheat the oven to 180°C (350°F) Gas 4.

Cover a plate with flour, season with a generous pinch of salt and drag the wing through the flour to evenly coat it on both sides, patting off any excess.

Put the floured wings on the prepared baking sheets with the thin meat side down (wings are thicker on one side than the other), and drizzle over a little oil, rub it all over the top side then turn the wing over and repeat.

Bake in the preheated oven for 15 minutes. The wing should be 55°C (130°F) at the thickest point when tested with a meat thermometer.

Meanwhile, heat the butter in a saucepan – the butter will begin to foam as the water particles in the butter boil off. As soon as the butter stops foaming the temperature will rise rapidly and you need to take it off the heat as soon as it starts to colour a light brown. There should be a distinctive hazelnut aroma at this stage. To halt the cooking, carefully squeeze a wedge of lemon into the butter.

To serve, simply place the wing on a warmed plate, pour over a generous portion of the hazelnut butter (*beurre noisette*), a small squeeze of lemon and a pinch of sea salt.

RED MULLET WITH SEAWEED

PREPARE: **10 MINUTES** COOK: **15 MINUTES** SERVES: **4**

Red mullet and snapper look stunning and need very little cooking for a delicious tasting fish dish. Edible seaweed is easy to source online and if it needs rehydrating, do so in lightly salted warm water, until it is tender enough to eat. The savoury or umami flavour of the seaweed works well with the texture and sweetness of cashews and the sharp flavour of tomato to create a balanced and tasty meal. I serve this as it comes but you could add new potatoes for a larger meal.

plain/all-purpose flour

salt

4 red mullet or snapper (each about 400–500 g/14–18 oz.) scaled, trimmed and gutted

vegetable oil

200 g/7 oz. edible seaweed, roughly chopped

100 g/⅔ cup unsalted cashew nuts, roughly chopped

12 cherry tomatoes

300 g/11 oz. samphire

butter

a baking sheet, greased or lined with baking parchment

Preheat the oven to 200°C (400°F) Gas 6.

Cover a plate with flour and season generously with salt. Roll the mullet in the seasoned flour then rub a little oil over the fish. Slice the sides of the fish twice at an angle, to allow even cooking and prevent the fish curling while cooking.

Stuff the cavities with the seaweed and cashew nuts. Place 3 tomatoes inside each fish.

Place the fish on the prepared baking sheet and bake in the preheated oven at for 10–12 minutes, until the fish is cooked through and just starting to colour.

Put the samphire in a frying pan/skillet set over a medium heat with a little butter. Fry for a couple of minutes then heap onto serving plates. Top with the baked mullet and dress with any seaweed and cashew mixture and tomatoes left on the baking sheet.

FLOUNDER FILLETS WITH TARRAGON SAUCE

PREPARE: **30 MINUTES**   COOK: **10 MINUTES**   SERVES: **4**

A simple tarragon sauce for fish is a classic combination of flavours – you can and I'm sure you will use this sauce again and again with all kinds of fish.

200 ml/¾ cup white wine

350 g/3 sticks butter

a bunch of fresh tarragon leaves, finely chopped

2 large potatoes, peeled and diced into 5-mm/¼-in. cubes

salt

150 g/1¼ cups frozen peas

150 g/3 cups spinach, washed and destalked

8 flounder fillets

2 lemons, 1 cut into wedges

Preheat the oven to 200°C (400°F) Gas 6.

Pour the wine into a saucepan and set over a medium heat. Add 200 g/1 stick plus 6 tablespoons of butter and simmer for a few minutes until the alcohol has boiled off; the smell of the sauce will become sweet when this happens. Add two-thirds of the chopped tarragon to the pan and keep over a gentle heat until you are ready to serve.

Cook the potatoes in a pan of boiling water for 5 minutes until they are just starting to crumble; drain and leave to dry in the colander for 5 minutes. Arrange on a baking sheet and dot with 50 g/3½ tablespoons of butter. Bake in the preheated oven for 5 minutes then turn, season with a little salt and bake for another few minutes, until browned and crispy.

Steam the peas and spinach, over the tarragon sauce to capture the flavours from the sauce. Season lightly with salt if needed.

Put the remaining butter in a large frying pan/skillet set over a medium heat. When the butter is melted and foaming, season lightly with salt and carefully place the flounder fillets in the pan, skin-side down, applying a little pressure to them using the flat of a fish slice, until the meat relaxes and the fillet lies flat in the pan. Continue cooking until the flesh is opaque two-thirds of the way through. Squeeze over a generous amount of lemon juice and cover. Take off the heat for 2–3 minutes.

Serve the flounder on a bed of spinach and peas, with the potatoes on the side, then spoon the sauce over and sprinkle with fresh tarragon leaves.

JOHN DORY WITH SAFFRON, CAULIFLOWER & MOCK SEAWEED

PREPARE: **10 MINUTES**   COOK: **30 MINUTES**   SERVES. **4**

John Dory is the most stunning looking fish. Legend has it that the dark spots on a John Dory were said to be St. Peter's thumb and finger prints. This recipe is a simple treatment of the fish. Poaching in fish stock infuses the fish with flavour and the saffron adds colour and a distinctive savouriness to the sauce which contrast with the strong crunch and saltiness of our mock seaweed. Mock seaweed is fun to make and tastes amazing; I eat it as a snack on its own.

1 small cauliflower

plain/all-purpose flour

butter

500 ml/2 cups Fish Stock (see page 11)

a large pinch of saffron threads

4 John Dory (each about 400 g/14oz. or 1 x 1.5-kg/13¼-lbs.), trimmed, scaled and gutted

200 ml/¾ cup double/heavy cream

MOCK SEAWEED

500 g/18 oz. kale, cleaned and roughly chopped

sea salt flakes

vegetable oil

Preheat the oven to 180°C (350°F) Gas 4.

To make the mock seaweed, put the kale, a generous teaspoon of sea salt flakes and enough oil to coat in a large resealable bag, toss together to coat. Arrange on a baking sheet and bake in the preheated oven for 10 minutes. Turn the kale and bake for another 5 minutes. It will be crunchy and salty when done.

Using a sharp knife or a mandoline, very thinly slice the cauliflower. Coat the cauliflower slices with flour and gently fry them in butter until they are translucent and slightly browned. Remove from the pan and set aside.

Bring the stock to a simmer in a large saucepan set over a medium heat. Add the saffron and continue to simmer for 5 minutes before adding the fish. Cover and simmer for 3 minutes for small fish, or 5 minutes for the large fish.

Carefully lift the John Dory from the pan using a fish slice and place on a plate surrounded by the mock seaweed and cauliflower. Add the cream to the remaining stock and bring back to simmer before pouring into a sauce jug to serve at the table.

SHELLFISH & CRUSTACEANS

Shellfish come in many shapes and sizes, from the cockles, mussels and clams (pipis) I used to collect as a kid, to stick-like razor clams and rough-textured barnacles, they are the tidal feeders that filter their food from the ocean. Wonderfully sustainable when farmed or harvested with care, shellfish are one of my go-to foods when I want a quick and tasty dish. The flavours from the Smoked Mussel Gratin (page 123) will amaze you. There is a reason I use mussels in so many dishes, and it's because they taste delicious and are cheap and sustainable. Scallop Chowder (page 133) is a favourite restaurant dish of mine. For extra fun, serve it in a hollowed out loaf of bread. Spaghetti Vongole (page 142) is a beautiful dish to serve, the epitome of good classic Italian cooking, using the very best ingredients.

The depth of flavours from crustaceans is unmatched by any animal in my opinion and I love to cook and eat them. Lobster was once seen as peasant food, nowadays it is often the most expensive dish on a menu. Well-priced lobster can be found in many supermarkets, and there are instructions for preparing cooked lobster on page 152 so don't be scared to buy it whole. If a good Lobster Bisque (page 155) was my last meal I would be very happy. I won MasterChef cooking a crab dish and a version of the Crab Thermidor (page 151) that is included here. Try it with lobster, too, the recipe works for either but trust your tastebuds when it comes to seasoning the dish. Who couldn't smile at the thought of a Prawn Dog with Seafood Ketchup (page 148)? A good seafood curry takes some beating and my Kashmir Prawn Curry (page 147) is no exception: creamy, coconuty with cashews and tomatoes; while a Langoustine Cocktail (page 156) makes a stunning appetizer.

SMOKED MUSSEL GRATIN

PREPARE: **45 MINUTES** COOK: **15 MINUTES** SERVES: **4**

This is a version of the mussel gratin I serve in my restaurant. It is rich and sumptuous and is always a popular choice for guests. Take care not to over smoke the mussels as it will overpower their delicate flavour. If you do not have a barbecue, simply mix canned smoked mussels with shelled freshly cooked mussels to achieve a rich, smokey flavour.

2 slices white bread

salt

100 g/1⅓ cups grated Parmesan cheese

2 kg/4½ lbs. mussels, cleaned and de-bearded

200 ml/¾ cup white wine

1 litre/1¾ pints Shellfish Stock (see page 11)

100 g/1⅓ cups grated cheddar cheese

2 teaspoons Dijon mustard

100 ml/⅓ cup double/heavy cream

a dash of Tabasco

2 teaspoons fish sauce (Nam Pla), to taste

wood smoking chips, soaked for at least 10 minutes

Preheat the oven to 180°C (350°F) Gas 4.

Put the bread slices directly onto the shelf of the preheated oven and bake for 5 minutes, until it is crispy and golden. Cool then place in a resealable bag. Crush to coarse breadcrumbs using a rolling pin, add a generous pinch of salt and ½ tablespoon of the Parmesan, reseal the bag and shake to combine.

Keep the oven on.

Put the mussels, white wine and 200 ml/¾ cup of the stock in a large saucepan set over a medium heat. Cover and cook until the mussels just open. Strain the mussels, reserving the liquor for later. Take the meat out of the shells and set on an ovenproof plate, discarding the shells.

To smoke the mussels, you will need to use a baking sheet that will fit under the lid of the barbecue. Cover the baking sheet with a 2.5-cm/1-in. layer of crumpled foil, then place the plate of mussel meat on top (the foil is to insulate the mussels from the direct heat of the barbecue).

Sprinkle the soaked wood chips generously over the top of the preheated barbecue. Place the baking sheet with the mussels on the barbecue, close the lid and leave to smoke for 5 minutes (or longer if the smoke is not particularly intense).

Pour the reserved cooking liquor from the mussels and the remaining stock into a large saucepan set over a medium heat. Bring to a simmer, then grate and whisk in the remaining Parmesan and cheddar cheeses, the Dijon mustard, double/heavy cream and Tabasco. Taste and add a little fish sauce until the sauce is seasoned to your liking.

Divide the smoked mussels between individual ovenproof dishes. Pour over enough sauce to almost cover them, then sprinkle with the breadcrumb mixture. Bake in the still-warm oven for 10–12 minutes until hot and bubbling and the breadcrumbs are lightly browned. Serve at once.

Tip: If you don't have time to smoke the mussels, replace them with 200 g/7 oz. of canned mussels plus 1 kg/35 oz. of fresh mussels cooked as above.

ROCKPOOL SOUP WITH SQUID, CLAMS, MUSSELS, SEAWEED & SAMPHIRE

PREPARE: **30 MINUTES**   COOK: **30 MINUTES**   SERVES: **4**

A wonderfully dramatic dish and a great talking point at the table, this dish should be reminiscent of childhood holidays spent rockpooling at the beach. Have fun with the presentation by including some shells and using dark coloured crockery (as pictured) to mimic a rockpool. Instead of squid, you could use razor clams or winkles, or even include a whole cooked crab claw.

60 g/3 cups dried seaweed

400 g/14 oz. surf clams

800 g/28 oz. mussels, cleaned and de-bearded

200 ml/¾ cup white wine

2 large brown onions, peeled and finely diced

4 garlic cloves, peeled and thinly sliced

butter, for frying

50 g/1 cup fresh flat-leaf parsley

4 green chillies/chiles, thinly sliced

1 litre/1¾ pints Fish Stock (see page 11)

a pinch of sea salt flakes

4 small squid or 2 large squid, cleaned and portioned (see page 161)

200 g/7 oz. fresh samphire

To rehydrate the dried seaweed, put it in a bowl of cold salted water and set in the fridge for 2 hours. Trim off any thick or coarse pieces and discard.

Put the clams and mussels into a hot saucepan set over a medium heat, then add the white wine, cover and cook until they just open. Strain the clams and mussels, reserving the liquor for later. Remove the clams from their shells. Put the clam meat and mussels to one side.

Put the onion and garlic in a frying pan/skillet set over a gentle heat with the butter. Fry until they are fragrant and translucent. Add the parsley, chilies/chiles, stock and reserved clam liquor, and bring to the boil. Reduce the heat and simmer for 15–20 minutes. Season with salt, then strain to leave a clear, pale green liquor, or consommé.

Add the squid to a hot dry frying pan/skillet set over a high heat. Cook for 30 seconds, turn over and cook for a further 30 seconds. Add one-quarter of the consommé, the clams and mussels, then cover.

Dress your serving bowls with the seaweed and samphire, then add the squid, clams and mussels. You can either add the hot consommé to the bowls and serve, or, for a more dramatic effect, put the consommé in small jugs and pour into the bowls at the table.

MUSSELS THREE WAYS

PREPARE: **10 MINUTES**   COOK: **10 MINUTES**   EACH SERVES: **4**

To be honest, mussels work well with most alcoholic drinks, but here are three variations to try. Cider adds a lovely apple sweetness that works well with the mussels and samphire adds a wonderful light salty flavour; wine is the classic accompaniment and is best served simply with crusty bread; while ale is hearty and the extra garlic adds depth and body to the dish.

WITH CIDER & SAMPHIRE

1 brown onion, peeled and finely chopped

1 tablespoon vegetable oil

1 garlic clove, peeled and finely chopped

1 kg/35 oz. mussels

300 ml/1¼ cups cider

150 g/5½ oz. samphire

50 ml/3½ tablespoons double/heavy cream

WITH WINE (MEUNIÈRE)

2 red onions, peeled and finely chopped

1 tablespoon vegetable oil

1 garlic clove, peeled and finely chopped

1 kg/35 oz. mussels

200 ml/¾ cup white wine mixed with 100 ml/⅓ cup water

50 ml/3½ tablespoons double/heavy cream

WITH ALE & GARLIC

1 brown onion, peeled and finely chopped

1 tablespoon vegetable oil

3 garlic cloves, peeled and finely chopped

1 kg/35 oz. mussels

300 ml/1¼ cups ale

50 ml/3½ tablespoons double/heavy cream

For each recipe, in a large pan set over a gentle heat, sweat off the onion in the vegetable oil until translucent. Then add the garlic (the garlic will burn if you add it at the same time as the onion) and continue to cook gently for another couple of minutes.

Meanwhile, prepare the mussels by gently rinsing under cold water and removing any 'beards'. Use a table knife (or any blunt knife) to scrape any loose barnacles off the shells and grab the beard with it to pull it off.

For mussels with cider and samphire, remove any hard stalks from the samphire, then finely chop.

Put all of the mussels into a saucepan set over a high heat, add the alcohol and cover. Bring to the boil for 2–3 minutes until the mussels have opened – don't overboil or you'll have rubbery mussels.

Take off the heat, add the double/heavy cream and samphire (if using), stir and spoon the mussels into big bowls (there's going to be a little grit at the bottom of the pan, so don't serve the last spoonful of the sauce).

Serve with generous hunks of bread to mop-up the delicious juices.

Note: Like most seafood, mussels should have no aroma; if they smell overly fishy or of ammonia, don't eat them. Discard any mussels that will not close when tapped gently, before cooking, as well as those which do not open after cooking.

OYSTERS MIGNONETTE

PREPARE: **20 MINUTES**   SERVES: **4**

This is the classic way to eat raw oysters, the sourness of the vinegar, bitterness of the raw onion and a little sweetness balance the savoury and saltiness of the oyster to create a mouthful of flavour. To eat a raw oyster, press it to the roof of your mouth with your tongue and let the soft tissue melt away leaving just the muscle to be chewed.

24 oysters
1 shallot, finely chopped
1 teaspoon caster/granulated sugar
120 ml/½ cup red wine vinegar
salt
170 g/1 cup crushed ice

Begin by preparing the oysters following the instructions below.

Make the mignonette sauce by whisking the shallot, sugar and red wine vinegar together.

Add a pinch of salt to the crushed ice and stir to combine. Arrange on serving plates and place eight oysters in their shells on each. Pour the sauce into a dipping bowl and serve with the oysters.

HOW TO SHUCK OYSTERS

1 Use a proper oyster knife with a shield to protect your hands and hold the oyster using a tea towel.

2 Insert the knife into the pointy hinge of the shell and twist the knife to open the hinge.

3 Slide the knife under the shell, cut the joining muscle close to the top of the flat side of the shell then lift off the top of the shell.

4 Cut the bottom of the muscle from the lower part of the shell.

5 Pick out any little pieces of shell that might have broken off into the oyster and pour away any excess water.

6 Carefully turn the oyster over in the shell and it is ready for serving.

1   2   3   4   5

Take 8 of the oyster shells and place each on a little crumpled foil on a baking sheet so they are level and supported. Place a dessert spoon of the spinach leaves in the bottom of each shell then the oyster on top. Drizzle a generous amount of hollandaise sauce over the top then a sprinkle of cheese.

Bake under a hot grill/broiler for 3–4 minutes until the cheese is browned.

To serve, use spinach or salt to support the oyster shells on the plates, so they don't wobble.

BEER BATTERED OYSTERS

PREPARE: **20 MINUTES**   COOK: **5 MINUTES**   SERVES: **4**

I was lucky growing up in New Zealand, where my local chip shop would always have battered oysters (pictured opposite) on the menu. Custard powder in the batter may seem strange but trust me it works, it gives a lovely colour and sweetness to balance the flavour of the stout.

200 g/1⅔ cups plain/all-purpose flour

200 ml/¾ cup stout beer, chilled

½ teaspoon baking powder

1 teaspoon custard powder

a pinch of salt

vegetable oil

24 oysters, shucked (see page 128) and shells reserved

100 ml/⅓ cup Aioli (see page 60)

In a bowl, whisk together 100 g/¾ cup of the flour, the beer, baking powder, custard powder and a pinch of salt.

Pour enough oil into a small pan to a depth of about 2 cm/¾ in. and heat to 180°C (350°F). It's at the right temperature when a drop of the batter sizzles and cooks to a crunchy texture in 1 minute.

Cover a large plate with the remaining flour and roll the oysters in it to coat them, then dip them in the beer batter mixture.

Carefully place the oysters in the hot oil and cook for no more than 2 minutes, turning once while cooking, until lightly browned and crunchy.

Serve the battered oysters in their shells with aioli.

OYSTERS ROCKEFELLER

PREPARE: **20 MINUTES**   COOK: **5 MINUTES**   SERVES: **4**

This was the favourite dish, pictured opposite, of Monica, a lady who lived next door to my first restaurant The Wild Garlic. By lightly cooking the oysters, you keep the flavour, but it stops the fear of eating something raw.

150 g/1½ cups spinach

butter, for frying

salt

24 oysters

Hollandaise Sauce (see page 81)

50 g/½ cup grated emmental cheese

Prepare the oysters following the instructions on page 128. Remove the meat from the shell and set aside.

Fry the spinach with a little butter and a pinch of salt in a frying pan/skillet set over a medium heat until just wilted.

SCALLOP CHOWDER

PREPARE: **20 MINUTES**   COOK: **30 MINUTES**   SERVES: **4**

If there's one dish that set me on my way to winning MasterChef this was it, a seafood chowder served in a bread bowl really set the scene for my type of cooking; fun, delicious and not at all pretentious. This is inspired by a chowder in a bread bowl I had over 20 years ago on Pier 39 in San Francisco and, like all great meals, it's never been forgotten. This version uses scallops, but do use mussels or other shellfish as a substitute.

16 scallops (or 200 g/7 oz. scallop meat)

2 leeks, trimmed and thinly sliced

3 potatoes, peeled and diced

2 brown onions, peeled and finely chopped

200 g/7 oz. monkfish tail, trimmed and diced into bite-sized pieces

1 litre/1¾ pints Shellfish Stock (see page 11), preferably made with scallop frills

a small bunch of fresh chives

4 small round loaves of soda or sourdough bread (optional)

Prepare the scallops by slicing the meat into 5-mm/¼-in. thick discs.

Put the vegetables into a pan of boiling water and cook until the potatoes are cooked through. Drain, reserving the liquor, and set aside half of the vegetables.

Pour the stock over the remaining vegetables in the pan and blend to a thick sauce using a handheld electric blender. Add a little of the vegetable cooking water if needed, to achieve a consistency of double/heavy cream. Bring this base to a low simmer and season to taste.

In a hot dry non-stick frying pan/skillet set over a high heat, quickly colour the monkfish pieces for no more than 30 seconds.

Add the monkfish and remaining vegetables to the blended sauce and bring to a low simmer. Add the sliced scallops, stir to combine and serve with a sprinkle of finely chopped chives over the top.

Tip: To serve the chowder in a bread bowl, cut a cup-sized circle in the top of the bread rolls and dig out the soft inner, leaving about 2–3 cm/1–1¼ in. of crust. Save the circle to use as a lid. Fill the bowls with the chowder and serve immediately with the lids on, a soup spoon and a bib!

GRILLED SCALLOPS WITH CHORIZO

PREPARE: **15 MINUTES**   COOK: **10 MINUTES**   SERVES: **4**

Scallops and chorizo make a wonderful combination as the heat of the chorizo goes well with the sweetness of fresh scallops, add some celeriac purée for a smooth yet slightly bitter and fragrant flavouring and this dish is a delight. Serve as an appetizer of three scallops in the shell.

1 small celeriac, peeled and diced

milk, to cover

salt and freshly ground black pepper

12 king scallops

200 g/7 oz. cooking chorizo, finely diced

a small bunch of fresh flat-leaf parsley

Put the celeriac in a saucepan set over a medium heat and pour over enough milk to just cover. Simmer for 15 minutes, then carefully remove the celeriac and transfer to a food processor. Blend the celeriac, adding some of the milk liquor to a thick creamy purée. Season with a generous pinch of salt and set aside.

Preheat the grill/broiler to 160°C (325°F) Gas 3.

Prepare the scallops by removing the meat and the roe, then cleaning out the scallop shells. Arrange the shells on a baking sheet, using a little crumpled foil as a base to stop them from rolling around.

In the bottom of each scallop shell, place ½ tablespoon of celeriac purée, 1 scallop, 1 teaspoon of diced chorizo and a pinch of salt.

Place them under the preheated grill/broiler and bake for 8–10 minutes. Your scallops should be just starting to brown on top.

Serve 3 scallop shells on each plate with a generous sprinkle of chopped parsley on top.

Tip: I sometimes arrange a bed of salad leaves on the plate to hold the shells upright.

SCALLOPS ST. JACQUES

PREPARE: **40 MINUTES** COOK: **15 MINUTES** SERVES: **4**

Scallops are called *Coquilles St. Jacques* in French and the same name is used for a traditional dish with white wine, served in the shell. My take on this dish uses a delicate mix of stock vegetables, white wine, Pernod and garlic with the scallop, encased in the shell and sealed with a pastry rim. Pay extra and use fresh-dived scallops, not only are they much cleaner and healthier than other scallops, they are sustainably caught, too.

1 carrot, peeled

1 celery stalk

1 onion, peeled

1 garlic clove, peeled

a pinch of salt

10 g/⅔ tablespoon butter

100 ml/¾ cup white wine

10 ml/2 teaspoons Pernod (or other aniseed-based liqueur)

50 ml/3½ tablespoons double/heavy cream

4 large hand-dived scallops

150 g/5½ oz. readymade puff pastry

1 egg, beaten

This recipe is all about perfect knife skills. Take your time and cut a dozen matchsticks of carrot, a dozen 4-mm/⅛-in. cubes of celery and a dozen 4-mm/⅛-in. squares of onion. Slice the garlic clove into 8 very thin slices.

Put all of the vegetable pieces and garlic in a small pan set over a very gentle heat with the butter and a tiny pinch of salt. Melt the butter and warm the vegetables for 15–20 minutes (they should not sizzle in the pan but just slowly become cooked through and translucent). Add the white wine and Pernod and bring to a low simmer for about 5 minutes to boil off the alcohol, then add the cream and take off the heat. Set aside to cool.

Preheat the oven to 180°C (350°F) Gas 4.

Prepare the scallops by removing the meat and the roe if it is a bright orange colour, then cleaning out the scallop shells. Set each element aside.

Roll out the pastry on a lightly floured surface to a rectangle about 30 x 20 cm/12 x 8 in. and cut into four long strips.

Place 1 scallop with the roe, if using, 3 carrot sticks, 3 celery cubes, 3 onion pieces and 2 slices of garlic in each shell. Spoon over the sauce until the shell is two-thirds full. Place the top on the shell and paint the edge with the beaten egg before wrapping the edge with the pastry strip to seal. Finally brush the pastry with the beaten egg. The scallops can be stored for up to 24 hours in the fridge at this stage.

Place the scallops on a baking sheet, using a little crumpled foil as a base to stop them from rolling around. Bake in the preheated oven for 12 minutes. Remove the scallops and rest for a few minutes before serving. Use some seaweed to support the shells on the plate.

WHELKS WITH GARLIC BUTTER

PREPARE: **5 MINUTES**   COOK: **10 MINUTES**   SERVES: **4**

Whelks are hugely underrated and sadly, in the United Kingdom, we export nearly all of them to Spain and France, where they're considered a delicacy. Be careful not to overcook whelks as they can get tough and chewy. This is a dish for eating with your fingers, as you need to hold the whelks quite firmly in order to prize the meat out so always serve with a generous supply of napkins.

200 g/¾ cup butter

4 garlic cloves, peeled and crushed

salt and freshly ground black pepper

1 kg/35 oz. whelks, cleaned

200 ml/¾ cup white wine

1 red onion, peeled and finely diced

4 mild red chillies/chiles, thinly sliced

a small bunch of fresh flat-leaf parsley, finely chopped

Put the butter in a small saucepan set over a gentle heat and melt until it just starts to foam. Add the garlic and immediately take off the heat. Add a small pinch of salt to season and set aside.

Put the whelks with the white wine, onion and 200 ml/¾ cup of water in a large saucepan set over a medium heat. Cover and bring to a simmer, then continue to simmer for 5 minutes.

Add the chillies/chiles, parsley and a generous pinch of salt and black pepper. Toss together to combine.

Spoon the whelks into serving bowls and serve with a side dish of the hot garlic butter, for dipping them into.

Tip: Serve this dish with plenty of napkins to hold the shells and small forks to extricate the whelks from them.

CLAMS WITH CAPER MAYONNAISE

PREPARE: **1 HOUR**   COOK: **20 MINUTES**   SERVES: **20**

This is a canapé dish I made on MasterChef, it looks fantastic as well as being tasty. The recipe is simple and one I still use in the restaurant as an amuse bouche today. You'll need to grow your own lemon thyme to get the flowers, although sometimes I use wild garlic or mint flowers depending on the season or just use a few lemon thyme leaves per each clam if you can't source the flowers. Making fresh mayonnaise is very rewarding and the flavour is fantastic, but if you are serving to the elderly, pregnant women or anyone with a diminished immune system then do use a store-bought pasteurized mayonnaise instead.

1 kg/35 oz. clams

200 ml/¾ cup first press rapeseed oil

1 duck egg

1 teaspoon white wine vinegar

a pinch of salt

100 g/10 tablespoons small capers

200 ml/¾ cups white wine

fresh lemon thyme flowers, to garnish

a 300-ml/1¼-cup capacity measuring jug/cup

Place the clams in fresh clean water for about an hour to purge them of any sand or grit. Discard any that are open.

Meanwhile, make the caper mayonnaise. Add the oil, egg, vinegar and salt to the jug/pitcher and wait for the egg to settle to the bottom, capture the egg under the base of a handheld electric blender but little or no oil. Now in short bursts of 2–3 seconds pulse to emulsify the oil and egg together to form mayonnaise. Continue pulsing and slowly draw it up through the jug/cup as the mayonnaise forms until all of the oil is combined and you have a thick, yellow mayonnaise.

Add approximately half of the capers to the mayonnaise and blend to mix them into the mayonnaise.

Place the purged clams in a large saucepan set over a medium heat. Add the wine and bring to a rapid boil until the clams are all open. Drain, reserving the liquor (this can be frozen and used to make a shellfish stock following the instructions on page 11 at another time). Set the clams aside to cool.

Place each open clam on a platter, add a ½ teaspoon of mayonnaise to each one. Add 2 capers, followed by a thyme flower and serve within 2 hours.

Tip: If you don't time to make the mayonnaise, use 250 ml/1 cup of store-bought mayonnaise.

SPAGHETTI VONGOLE

PREPARE: **5 MINUTES**   COOK: **15 MINUTES**   SERVES: **4**

A classic dish of fresh clams and pasta, this is a delight to make and it carries with it the essence of the sea. A great introduction to shellfish, my kids love this dish. For a little more money buy a good quality 'bronze-dyed' pasta (available online), this gives the pasta a rough texture which allows it to absorb the flavours of the sauce. The portion size is generous here, a proper one-dish meal for four. This dish works well too using mussels or other shellfish.

500 g/18 oz. small surf clams or cockles

1 teaspoon salt

400 g/14 oz. dried spaghetti

light olive oil

2 garlic cloves, peeled and thinly sliced

2 teaspoons dried chilli/hot red pepper flakes

50 g/¼ cup grated Parmesan cheese

freshly ground black pepper

Place the clams in fresh clean water for about an hour to purge them of any sand or grit. Discard any that are open.

Bring a large pan of water to the boil and add the salt.

Add the pasta to the water and stir to ensure it doesn't clump together. Simmer for 2 minutes less than the recommended cooking time.

Coat the bottom of a large frying pan/skillet to a depth of about 3-mm/⅛-in. and set over a gentle heat. Add the sliced garlic and chilli/hot red pepper flakes, heat gently till the garlic just begins to brown. Immediately remove from the heat and set aside.

Drain the pasta while still hot and add to the frying pan/skillet and turn it with a pair of tongs to coat well. Heat gently until the oiled pasta is steaming hot. Take off the heat, add the clams and cover, shake the pan a little to infuse the juices as the clams steam and open.

Serve with a little grated Parmesan and black pepper to taste.

STUFFED RAZOR CLAMS

PREPARE: **15 MINUTES** COOK: **5 MINUTES** SERVES: **4**

You want to cook razor clams as little as possible to preserve their delicate flavour. A little white wine sauce with the heat of a chilli/chile, Pernod and fresh saltiness of the samphire makes this a well-balanced but light dish. Use chopped parsley instead of samphire if it's out of season.

1 small red onion, peeled and finely chopped

25 g/1¾ tablespoons butter

175 ml/¾ cup white wine

12 razor clams

2 red chillies/chiles, chopped

200 g/7 oz. samphire, chopped

25 ml/1½ tablespoons Pernod (or other aniseed-based liqueur)

freshly ground black pepper

Cook the onion with the butter in a saucepan big enough to take all the razor clams set over a gentle heat, until translucent.

Pour in the wine and simmer for a couple of minutes to cook off the alcohol (you can smell when the alcohol is cooked-off, the smell goes from being acrid to being sweet).

Put the razor clams in their shells in the saucepan, cover and turn up the heat. The clams will cook and open in about 2 minutes. Take off the heat, remove the clams and set aside.

Add the chillies/chiles and samphire to the sauce, then the Pernod, and leave on a low heat to just simmer for a couple of minutes.

Chop the white clam meat into about 5-mm/¼-in. slices, discarding the rest.

Place the shells on plates and sprinkle the white meat evenly in the shells. Spoon the hot sauce over the top and finish with some black pepper.

KASHMIR PRAWN CURRY

PREPARE: **10 MINUTES** COOK: **50 MINUTES** SERVES: **4**

This is not meant to be an authentic Kashmir curry by any stretch. This is rather a description of what I think when I imagine a Kashmir curry: mild curry flavours, lots of nutty and fruit flavours, it's a bit 1970s with the bananas included but we all love it in my house. This is the curry my kids will eat every time and fight over the scraps, you can even kid yourself that it's healthy with the fruit in it. Use uncooked prawns if possible as there is usually a lot of water frozen with the cooked, frozen varieties that seeps into the dish when cooking.

2 brown onions, peeled and chopped

3 garlic cloves, peeled and chopped

2 x 5-cm/2½-in. pieces of fresh ginger, peeled and thinly sliced

vegetable oil, for frying

2 teaspoons Masala Spice Blend (see page 70)

1 teaspoons ground turmeric

200 g/2 cups ground cashew nuts

400 g/2 cups canned chopped tomatoes

50 g/⅓ cup sultanas/golden raisins

salt

300 g/1¾ cups long-grain rice

500 g/18 oz. uncooked peeled prawns/shrimp

1 firm banana, peeled and sliced into 5-mm/¼-in. rounds

1 teaspoon nigella/black onion seeds

2 tablespoons flaked/slivered almonds

1 tablespoon fennel seeds

Firstly let's make the base for the curry using the onions, garlic and ginger – if you like curry its worth making multiples of this base and freezing it. Put the onions, garlic and ginger in a large saucepan and just cover with water. Set over a gentle heat and bring to a low simmer for 30 minutes. Purée the mixture after cooking with a handheld electric blender. If you can, make this the day before and leave to infuse in the fridge overnight.

Cover the base of a large frying pan/skillet with a thin coating of oil and set over a medium heat. Once hot, add the masala spice blend and turmeric, then once the spices start to release their aroma, add the ground cashew nuts. Heat for a couple of minutes then add the base mixture, chopped tomatoes and sultanas/golden raisins and bring to a gentle simmer.

In another saucepan add 600 ml/2 cups of water and a pinch of salt and bring to a simmer over a medium heat. Add the rice, bring back to a simmer then take off the heat, cover and leave for 15 minutes, when the rice will be cooked.

Heat a little oil in a small saucepan set over a medium heat and add the almonds, nigella and fennel seeds. Warm until they start to pop and the almonds colour to a light golden brown. Remove from the heat and set aside.

Add prawns/shrimp to the sauce and simmer for 5 minutes then add the banana. Stir in carefully and after another 5 minutes, the curry should be ready to serve. Taste the sauce and add a little salt (about ½ teaspoon) to season.

Serve with the cooked rice and dress with a sprinkle of the toasted almonds, fennel and nigella seeds to add some flavour explosions and texture to the finished dish.

Tip: The fennel seeds may be too strong in flavour for some, so just leave them out. If you like your curry hotter in spice, then add a finely chopped red chilli/chile (or two) to the pan with the masala and turmeric spices.

PRAWN DOGS WITH SEAFOOD KETCHUP

PREPARE: **1 HOUR**   COOK: **2 MINUTES**   SERVES: **4**

How can any dish called Prawn Dogs not be fun? Use a soft finger roll to make a tasty alternative to the usual sausage-in-a-bun hot dog. I love using a dry rub of spices for food cooked on the barbecue, but do adjust the spicing and chilli/chile heat to suit your own taste (this is a fairly mild heat). Use the largest prawns you can buy and use the heads and shells to make the ketchup base. I've written the recipe allowing for two rolls each, in my experience it's impossible to only eat one!

16 extra-large/colossal prawns/shrimp, heads and shells on

8 white finger rolls, cut in half and spread with mayonnaise, to serve

dried onions, to serve

DRY RUB

2 teaspoons ground dried onion powder

1 teaspoon ground dried garlic powder

1 teaspoon smoked paprika

½ teaspoon cayenne powder

¼ teaspoon salt

¼ teaspoon ground white pepper

SEAFOOD KETCHUP

vegetable oil, for frying

1 brown onion, peeled and diced

2 garlic cloves, peeled and sliced

2 teaspoons dried chilli/hot red pepper flakes

800 g/4 cups canned chopped tomatoes

2 teaspoons celery salt

2 teaspoons caster/granulated sugar

1 teaspoon balsamic vinegar

½ teaspoon xanthan gum, to thicken (optional)

Prepare the prawns/shrimp in advance by removing the heads and shells and trimming out the waste line. Keep the heads and shells but discard the waste line. You can refrigerate the prepared prawns/shrimp for up to 48 hours.

Make the seafood ketchup well in advance so it has time to cool. Place the heads and shells of the prawns/shrimp in a hot dry pan set over a medium heat and cook until they start to catch and brown, add a splash of oil and the onion and stir to quickly cook the onion. Next add the garlic and chilli/hot red pepper flakes and continue to cook for about 30 seconds, continuously stirring so the garlic doesn't burn. Add the canned tomatoes with the remaining ketchup ingredients except for the xanthan gum, reduce the heat and keep at a low simmer for about 15 minutes. Blend the mixture to a purée using a handheld electric blender and pass through a fine mesh sieve/strainer set over a jug/pitcher to remove any lumps and shell fragments. If the resulting sauce is at all watery add the xantham gum, return to a low simmer and blend to fully combine it into the sauce. Xanthan gum can be found in the baking aisle in most supermarkets and is used as a thickening agent – it is far better than cornflour/cornstarch in my opinion.

Put all of the dry rub ingredients in an extra-large, sealable sandwich bag.

Add the prawns/shrimp to the bag with the dry rub mixture, seal and shake to coat well.

Place the prawns/shrimp over a scorching hot dry pan over a high heat or on a barbecue and cook for about 1 minute on each side, until they have coloured through.

Put 2 cooked prawns in each roll, cover with a generous dollop of ketchup and sprinkle with dried onions before serving.

CRAB THERMIDOR

PREPARE: **15 MINUTES**   COOK: **30 MINUTES**   SERVES: **2**

This is a variation of the Spider Crab Thermidor I cooked as my MasterChef winning main dish. This is not a true thermidor recipe, as we make the sauce using cream, rather than a flour-based roux. However, this is the one I prefer and that I serve in my restaurant because of its wonderful flavour and because it can be eaten by people with a gluten intolerance. The flavour of crab changes throughout the season and so accordingly, the seasoning for this dish must be adjusted (tailor the mustard, Tabasco etc.). Use the method below as a guide but trust your taste buds, this is not a dish of exact measurements.

600 ml/2½ cups unreduced Shellfish Stock (see page 11)

a few drops of Tabasco sauce

1 teaspoon English mustard powder

60 g/½ cup grated Gruyère cheese

salt and freshly ground black pepper, to season

100 ml/⅓ cup double/heavy cream

200 g/7 oz. white crab meat

200 g/7 oz. brown crab meat

4 crab shells (you should be able to buy these from a fishmonger)

100 g/2 cups spinach

100 g/3½ oz. samphire, woody bits discarded

1 lemon, cut into wedges

Put the stock in a saucepan set over a medium heat and simmer until it has reduced by about two-thirds.

Add the Tabasco, English mustard, half of the cheese and a pinch of salt and pepper. Taste and adjust the seasoning if necessary – it should be a spicy, slightly salty, seafood liquor.

Turn the heat down and add the double/heavy cream, then the crab meat and gently stir together. You should now have a thick stew. Take care not to overcook or overstir it as the crab meat is quite delicate.

Fill each crab shell about a quarter of the way up with spinach leaves, then spoon over the mixture so that the shells are full.

Scatter with the remaining cheese and place the filled shells under a hot grill/broiler for a few minutes until the cheese has melted.

Make a small pile of samphire on each serving plate and place the hot crab shell on top of it. Just before serving, sprinkle the crab with pepper and squeeze fresh lemon juice over the samphire.

Note: Crab meat needs to be handled with care. It should either be kept fridge-cold, or above 70°C (160°F). It's very important not to leave it sitting out of the fridge for any longer than is necessary.

LOBSTER SALAD

PREPARE: **15 MINUTES** COOK: **30 MINUTES** SERVES: **4**

Frozen cooked lobster is commonly available in supermarkets, usually from sustainable sources in Canada and Alaska and at a reasonable price. Lobster is a delicate flavour so you need to be careful not to overpower it with strong flavours. It is also easy to prepare with a little practice. This salad is a delicious alternative to the usual hot dishes we more commonly associate with lobster. It is a lovely summery appetizer but can also make fantastic canapés, served on toasts.

150 ml/½ cup mayonnaise

a small bunch of fresh dill

grated zest and freshly squeezed juice of 1 lemon

2 small cooked lobster

1 green apple, peeled and cut into matchstick pieces

2 mild red chillies/chiles, thinly sliced

1 iceberg lettuce, finely chopped

150 g/3 cups rocket/arugula leaves

freshly ground black pepper

To make the sauce, blend together the mayonnaise, half of the dill and the lemon zest in a jug/pitcher using a handheld electric blender.

Mix the lobster tail meat and sauce together in a large mixing bowl.

In a separate bowl, cover the apple with lemon juice to stop it going brown.

Mix the salad leaves together then mix through the apple, chillies/chiles and half of the lobster meat. Toss together to combine.

Divide the salad between 4 bowls then dress with the remaining lobster meat, the cracked lobster claws, remaining dill and pepper.

HOW TO PREPARE COOKED LOBSTER

1 Using the cross on the top of the head as a guide cut firmly through.

2 Bring the knife forwards to cut through the head fully.

3 Slice firmly through the tail lengthwise.

4 Remove the white meat from the body save any brown meat and roe for sauces and stocks. Twist off the claws and crack them on a hard surface using the back of a heavy knife, ready to eat.

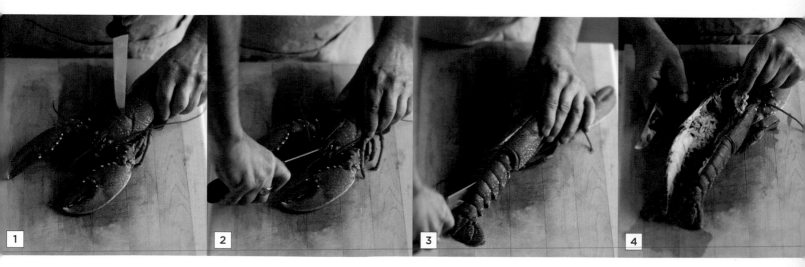

LOBSTER BISQUE

PREPARE: **45 MINUTES**   COOK: **1½ HOURS**   SERVES: **4**

Rather than an afterthought of what to do with lobster shells, for me, this dish is one of the best ways to cook with lobster. Give me the choice of a good lobster bisque or lobster meat on its own, I would choose lobster bisque every time. This requires some effort to get the flavour out of the shells. In the restaurant I have an industrial grade handheld electric blender but at home I use the end of a rolling pin, which does the job just as well but it's a little harder work. Traditionally, lobster bisque was made with the whole lobster, including the meat, to use up any damaged or imperfect lobster that couldn't be sold at market, so I use prawns as well as the lobster shells to give more balance to the broth. As with any shellfish recipes, the intensity of flavour will change with the seasons, so the measurements are approximate and will need adjusting to taste.

the shells of 2 lobsters

vegetable oil, to drizzle

200 ml/¾ cups white wine

200 g/7 oz. frozen prawns/shrimps, shells on

1 brown onion, peeled and finely chopped

2 carrots, finely chopped

2 celery stalks, finely chopped

140 g/5 oz. canned tomato purée/paste

40 ml/3 tablespoons Pernod Ricard

40 ml/3 tablespoons brandy

2 teaspoons smoked paprika/pimentón

50 ml/3½ tablespoons double/heavy cream

freshly squeezed juice of ½ lemon

¼ teaspoon salt

Preheat the oven to 160°C (325°F) Gas 3.

Place the lobster shells on a roasting pan, drizzle with a little oil and turn them with a spoon to coat well. Drain off any excess oil and roast in the preheated oven for 20 minutes.

Transfer the roasted shells to a large saucepan and set aside.

Deglaze the roasting pan by adding 800 ml/3⅓ cups of water and the white wine. Set over a medium heat and bring to a simmer whilst scraping at the bottom of the pan with a flat wooden spatula to incorporate all those lobster flavours that have become stuck to the bottom.

Carefully break the lobster shells into tiny pieces using the end of a rolling pin.

Pour the mixture from the roasting pan into the saucepan with the broken shells. Add the prawns/shrimp, onion, carrot and celery and bring to a low simmer, then reduce the heat so that it is below a simmer but still hot. Cover and keep at this temperature for 1 hour.

Meanwhile, cook the tomato purée/paste in a small non-stick frying pan/skillet set over a gentle heat for 2–3 minutes.

Blend the ingredients in the saucepan together using a handheld electric blender, then strain through a fine mesh sieve/strainer into a jug/pitcher (I like to use a muslin cloth/cheesecloth within the sieve/strainer to catch any bits). Discard the waste and pour the mixture back into the saucepan. Add the cooked tomato purée/paste, the Pernod, brandy and paprika/pimentón and bring to a low simmer, uncovered, until the volume has reduced by about one-quarter. Add the double/heavy cream, lemon juice and salt. Stir and serve.

Tips: Traditionally lobster bisque is made with chicken stock. I prefer the purity of this recipe as it is but if you would like a richer flavour, substitute the water for unreduced chicken stock. Save the lobster shells each time you cook with lobster by storing in the freezer until you have enough to make a bisque.

LANGOUSTINE COCKTAIL

PREPARE: **10 MINUTES**
COOK: **5 MINUTES** SERVES: **4**

**A slight twist on the classic
prawn/shrimp cocktail, this
is a bit 1980s but if I ever
put this dish on the restaurant
menu, it's always a top-seller.
I love these flavours together
and the theatre of langoustines
makes this fantastic fun.**

200 ml/²/₃ cup mayonnaise

150 ml/²/₃ cup Seafood Ketchup (see page 148)

50 g/5 tablespoons capers

a small bunch of fresh rocket/arugula leaves

50 g/2 oz. samphire

1 iceberg lettuce

salt

170 g/1 cup crushed ice

16 cooked large prawns/shrimp, peeled

8 cooked langoustines

1 lemon, cut into wedges

First, make the cocktail sauce by mixing the mayonnaise, ketchup and capers together in a small bowl.

Prepare the salad by mixing the rocket/arugula, samphire and sliced lettuce together in a large mixing bowl.

Add a pinch of salt to the crushed ice and stir to combine. Mix a small amount of the salted crushed ice through the salad to keep it fresh and crisp.

Arrange layers of salad and sauce in large serving glasses, with a couple of prawns in each layer of sauce. Top with sauce and two langoustines hanging over the edge of the glass. Serve immediately with a wedge of lemon.

Tip: If you don't have time to make the Seafood Ketchup, use 100 ml/⅓ cup of store-bought ketchup mixed with a splash of Tabasco and a squeeze of lemon juice.

SQUID & OCTOPUS

Squid is one of the most sustainable seafoods reaching maturity in little more than a year and it makes for great eating. The rule I always remember for cooking squid and octopus, is '30 seconds or 3 hours', reinforcing the times needed to cook it properly. Both squid and octopus benefit from freezing as it tenderizes the flesh, making it easier to handle.

Salt & Pepper Squid (page 169) is really tasty and is literally a 30-second dish as you can do all the preparation work in advance. Sweet Chilli Squid (page 162) is very similar in terms of cooking speed. It is a restaurant dish that always delights but you need to serve it immediately – in the restaurant I wouldn't start cooking squid until there is a waiter standing by, ready to whisk the plates straight to the table. The recipe for sweet chilli sauce is very simple and the result is so delicious you may never buy bottled sauce again.
Try Squid Ink Risotto (page 165) for a dramatic looking dish that tastes amazing or Barbecue Octopus with Grilled Lemons (page 173) for something very different in summer. In the cooler months a Slow-cooked Octopus & Chorizo Stew (page 170) simmering away or the roasting of the Spelt-stuffed Squid (page 166) will have everybody asking when dinner is

TEMPURA SQUID

PREPARE: **5 MINUTES** COOK: **5 MINUTES** SERVES: **2-4**

Tempura is a lighter form of battered squid. It's light and delicious and almost too easy to make. A great alternative to fish and chips, try it served with some raw vegetables on a hot day.

2 medium squid

vegetable oil, for frying

100 g/¾ cup plain/all-purpose flour

50 g/½ cup cornflour/cornstarch

10 g/1 tablespoon baking powder

100 ml/⅓ cup chilled sparkling water

salt and freshly ground black pepper

Sweet Chilli Sauce or Aioli, to serve (see pages 162 and 60)

Begin by preparing the squid following the instructions below, then cut the body into bite-sized portions.

Preheat a deep-fat fryer to 180°C (350°F) or fill a deep saucepan with oil and set over a medium heat to warm through.

Make the batter by stirring together the flour, cornflour/cornstarch and baking powder to a thick paste with a little sparkling water in a large mixing bowl. When ready to cook add the remaining chilled sparkling water to make a thin paste. Add the squid pieces to the batter then carefully place in the hot oil in the fryer and cook for 2 minutes. Remove the squid from the fryer and drain on paper towels for a few seconds, sprinkle with a little salt and pepper and serve immediately with a dip of either sweet chilli sauce or aioli.

Tip: Drop a little batter into the oil to test if it is hot enough. It should fizz and cook in 20 seconds. It will brown if the oil is too hot and stay soft if too cool.

HOW TO PREPARE SQUID

1 Gently pull the head away from the body taking the milky white intestines with it and cut off the tentacles from the head.

2 Squeeze out the beak-like mouth from the centre of the tentacles, cut away and discard.

3 Reach into the body and pull out the plastic-like quill and any soft white roe.

4 Scrape the outside of the head clean, removing any skin.

5 Pull off the two fins from either side of the body, slice the head open and wash the pouch with water.

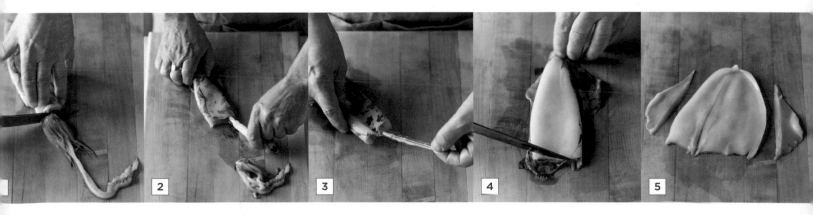

SWEET CHILLI SQUID

PREPARE: **30 MINUTES** COOK: **2 MINUTES** SERVES: **2-4**

The best advice I can give you for cooking squid is to do so for 30 seconds or 3 hours, anything in between will give you tough and chewy meat. Squid cooked properly is stunning to eat. This is one of my favourite dishes to cook in the restaurant but requires a waiter to be standing by as it has only a 30-second cooking process and then needs to be served straight away. I serve it on top of a salad to collect the delicious sweet and hot sauce from cooking. You'll need to open an outside door or have good ventilation when making the sauce as the chilli and vinegar are pungent to say the least! The final result is so much better than any store-bought sauce that it's well worth it.

200 g/4 cups mixed salad leaves

2 limes, 1 cut into wedges and 1 cut in half

2 tablespoons sesame oil

200 g/7 oz. squid meat, cleaned and chopped into small, bite-sized pieces (see page 161)

a small bunch of fresh coriander/cilantro, to garnish

SWEET CHILLI SAUCE

150 ml/$^2/_3$ cup white wine vinegar

100 g/$^1/_2$ cup caster/granulated sugar

2-4 red Thai chillies/chiles

2 garlic cloves, peeled and crushed

Begin by making the sweet chilli sauce. Combine the vinegar, sugar and chillies/chiles in a small saucepan (I would recommend using 2 chillies/chiles for the first time you make the sauce, that's plenty hot enough for me). Set the pan over a medium heat and simmer until it reduces by one-third. This will dampen the pungency of the vinegar and the sauce will be just beginning to thicken. Leave for 5 minutes to cool a little, then stir through the garlic. Set aside to allow the flavours to infuse and the sauce to cool.

Have bowls of salad leaves prepared with a wedge of lime to go on top of each one.

Set a non-stick frying pan/skillet over a high heat and add the oil. When the oil starts to smoke, carefully add the squid pieces to the pan. Cook for 20 seconds then stir quickly, the squid should be starting to change colour to a solid white (this may take a couple of minutes if using frozen squid pieces). Add the sweet chilli sauce and stir very quickly to combine, the sauce should bubble in the heat. Remove from the heat and immediately squeeze the lime over the pan to reduce the heat, stir to combine and serve on top of the salad, placing a wedge of lime on top of each serving.

Garnish with a few coriander/cilantro leaves, serve and eat straight away. The whole process should take no more than 2 minutes. Ready, set, go!

SQUID INK RISOTTO

PREPARE: **10 MINUTES** COOK: **20 MINUTES** SERVES: **4**

Wonderful comfort food and stunning to look at. The perfect risotto should hold its shape when placed on the plate but have just enough liquidity to settle into a flattened plate of food when the plate is tapped on the table. A chef friend, who also happens to hold a Michelin star, swears he can taste the difference if a risotto has not been stirred with a wooden spoon; on that basis, I always use one when cooking a risotto.

4 small squid

600 ml/2½ cups Fish or Shellfish Stock (see page 11)

½ cucumber, peeled

white wine vinegar, to cover

3–4 teaspoons caster/granulated sugar

olive oil, for frying

1 brown onion, peeled and finely diced

2 garlic cloves, peeled and thinly sliced

300 g/1½ cups arborio rice

4 x 16-g/⅟₂-oz. packets concentrated squid ink (available online)

200 ml/¾ cup white wine

a pinch of salt

a small bunch of fresh dill

80 g/1¼ cups grated Parmesan cheese

a knob of butter

Prepare the squid following the instructions up to step 4 on page 161, then instead of opening out the head, clean and slice it into rounds.

Pour stock into a saucepan set over a medium heat and bring to a simmer before adding the squid. Poach for 2 minutes until just cooked, then remove from the pan using a slotted spoon and set aside.

Make ribbons of cucumber with a peeler, then put the ribbons in a separate pan. Just cover with vinegar, then add an equal amount of water and a few teaspoons of sugar and bring to a simmer over a medium heat. Remove as soon as the mixture simmers and set aside.

Coat the base of a frying pan/skillet with a little oil and set over a very low heat. Add the onion and garlic and cook until just translucent. Add the rice and cook until the rice is covered with oil and starts to go opaque. Now add the squid ink and mix it in (with a wooden spoon), then add the wine and simmer until the wine is nearly all absorbed. While stirring constantly, add the stock a ladleful at a time, stirring until absorbed each time. Add a pinch of salt and continue cooking on a low simmer until the rice is cooked and has just a little bite; there should be no excess liquid. Stir in the Parmesan and butter.

Serve with a few ribbons of pickled cucumber on top, the squid and a sprinkle of finely chopped dill.

SPELT-STUFFED SQUID

PREPARE: **2 HOURS 30 MINUTES** COOK: **20 MINUTES** SERVES: **4**

Spelt is an old-fashioned grain, similar to barley, which makes a superb alternative to risotto rice and holds its texture well to preserve a firmness to the bite. Squid bodies stuffed with risotto are a classic dish; this is my take on it and it uses the spelt to enable a tasty dish than can be stored in the fridge for several days ready to bake.

4 medium squid, cleaned

200 ml/¾ cup white wine

500 ml/2 cups Fish Stock (see page 11)

2 carrots, finely diced

2 celery stalks, finely diced

2 red onions, peeled and finely diced

300 g/2 cups pearled spelt

salt and freshly ground black pepper, to season

50 g/3½ tablespoons butter

2 red chillies/chiles

a small bunch of fresh flat-leaf parsley

50 g/¾ cup grated Parmesan cheese

freshly ground black pepper

1 lemon, cut into wedges, to serve

Prepare the squid following the instructions up to step 4 on page 161, then instead of opening out the head, clean and place a wooden spoon handle inside them. Cut three slices at an angle through one side of the body, using the spoon handle stopping you from cutting all of the way through the squid. Cut the legs into small pieces.

Pour the wine and stock into a saucepan set over a gentle heat. Add the carrots, celery and half of the onion and bring to a low simmer. Add the prepared squid to the pan and keep at a low simmer for 2 hours, topping up with a little water if it starts to reduce in volume.

Remove the squid bodies and set aside. Add the spelt and continue to simmer, taste the liquor and add a little salt if needed. The spelt will cook in 20 minutes, check it is soft to eat but retains a little bite. Drain and discard any excess liquid.

Stir in the remaining onion, the butter, chillies/chiles and parsley leaves. Save the parsley stalks and chop them finely, to garnish.

Stuff the reserved squid bodies with the spelt mixture and chill in the fridge – they can be kept refrigerated for several days like this.

Preheat the oven to 200°C (400°F) Gas 6.

Put the stuffed squid on a baking sheet and bake in the preheated oven for 15 minutes, the body should just be starting to colour and the spelt should be heated through. Remove from the oven, sprinkle with grated Parmesan and rest for 5 minutes while the Parmesan melts and the temperature of the spelt evens out.

Serve simply on a plate with a wedge of lemon, sprinkled with the chopped parsley stems and a little black pepper. The spelt should spill out of the body and use some of the reserved, cooked chopped legs to decorate the plate.

SALT & PEPPER SQUID

PREPARE: **30 MINUTES**
COOK: **5 MINUTES** SERVES: **2-4**

Salt and pepper squid is becoming the default way to cook squid as the heat and salt work well with the tasty meat of squid. Usually battered but, for me, the batter disguises the flavour so my recipe relies on the spices and oils for flavour and is a lighter and fresher dish than those that batter.

2 medium squid
vegetable oil, for frying
3–4 teaspoons sesame oil
1 small red chilli/chile, thinly sliced
1 teaspoon ground black pepper
1 teaspoon ground Sichuan pepper
1 garlic clove, peeled and thinly sliced
1 spring onion/scallion, thinly sliced
1 teaspoon sea salt flakes
a small bunch of fresh coriander/cilantro
1 lime, cut into wedges

Prepare the squid following the instructions on page 161, then cut the body into rectangles and score the inside in a small (5-mm/¼-in.) diamond pattern.

Cover the base of the frying pan/skillet with vegetable oil (about 2 mm/⅛ in. deep) and add a few teaspoons of sesame oil. Heat the oil over a medium heat until it sizzles when a slice of chilli/chile is added to it. Add the sliced chilli/chile with both peppers and let them sizzle for a few seconds, then add the squid, garlic and spring onion/scallion. Stir quickly to cook the squid until coloured (no more than about 30 seconds – that's all it needs).

Drain on paper towels to absorb any excess oil, sprinkle with the salt and toss before placing onto hot plates. Serve with some coriander/cilantro leaves and a wedge of lime.

SLOW-COOKED OCTOPUS & CHORIZO STEW

PREPARE: **20 MINUTES** COOK: **1 HOUR** SERVES: **4**

Slow-cooked octopus is a delight to eat, full of flavour and very tender. The combination of octopus and chorizo works really well together and the mussels and white beans make this a satisfying and comforting dish.

vegetable oil, for frying

2 onions, peeled and finely diced

salt

2 garlic cloves, peeled and crushed

100 g/3½ oz. cooking chorizo

500 g/18 oz. octopus, cleaned and portioned

200 ml/¾ cup Fish Stock (see page 11)

410 g/2 cups canned cannellini beans

200 g/1¼ cups cherry tomatoes

300 g/11 oz. mussels

Put a few teaspoons of oil in a medium saucepan and set over a gentle–medium heat. Gently cook the chopped onion in the oil with a pinch of salt, until translucent. Add the garlic and continue to cook for 2 minutes more.

Finely chop half of the chorizo and add it to the pan with the octopus. Pour over the fish stock and bring to a simmer. Leave to simmer for 45 minutes, allowing the stock to reduce by two-thirds of its volume, but still enough to just cover the octopus.

Add the cannellini beans and cherry tomatoes, cover and bring back to a simmer for about 10 minutes. The stew can be chilled and kept for a couple of days in the fridge at this point.

When ready to serve, bring the stew to low simmer, adding the remaining chorizo, sliced into thin rounds with the mussels. Cover and steam until the mussels open. Serve in bowls with plenty of fresh bread to mop up the juices.

BARBECUE OCTOPUS WITH GRILLED LEMONS

PREPARE: **15 MINUTES** MARINATE: **12 HOURS**
COOK: **5 MINUTES** SERVES: **4**

Octopus are delicious and dramatic to serve. This is a simple barbecue recipe that is best cooked outside as it is very smoky – the results are fun and a great talking point over conventional barbecue fare. Prepare the octopus and use the legs cleaned of any hard 'suckers'. Resist the temptation to cook the octopus for more than a couple of minutes or it will be like eating rubber, one minute on each side is plenty of cooking time.

8 lemons

250 ml/1 cup plain yogurt

2 teaspoons coriander seeds

2 teaspoons ground cumin seeds

1 teaspoon ground turmeric

1 teaspoon allspice mix

2 teaspoons caster/granulated sugar

the legs of 1 large octopus (about 1 kg/ 35 oz.), cleaned and portioned

Begin by making the marinade. Mix the juice and zest of 4 of the lemons with the yogurt and spices in a mixing bowl. Coat the octopus legs with the marinade, cover and set in the fridge to chill overnight.

The next day, slice the remaining lemons into three slices each, sprinkle with a little sugar and set on the barbecue (or large ridged stovetop grill pan if cooking indoors) for 2–3 minutes until dark grill marks are formed. Turn the lemons over to cook the other side and add the octopus legs to the barbecue or pan. Turn the legs after 1 minute and cook the other side in the same way.

Serve the legs immediately with the grilled lemons – these can be squeezed over, or eaten with the legs.

Tip: You can serve the octopus legs on their own, with a bowl of salad or in bread rolls to make an octopus hotdog in the same way as the Prawn Dogs with Seafood Ketchup on page 148.

INDEX

ACKNOWLEDGMENTS

And finally, thanks for the help and support; this book is very much a collaboration with my wife Amanda who helps with recipe development, suggestions, ideas, writing and testing. Without her patience and support I would never have taken the leap into the world of food, I would have remained just another unhappy and unfulfilled corporate manager, thank you Amanda.

Recipes are never one person's ideas; many of these are versions of classics with origins in classical cooking. I've tried to make the recipes as approachable as possible and the instructions practical to follow.

Many of the chefs I've worked with have inspired me. From my own kitchens I have to thank, Dan B., Katy, Terry, Song and Heather, who have been my main kitchen and restaurant colleagues over the last five years. I also need to thank John Torode and Gregg Wallace along with the amazing Karen Ross and the production team from MasterChef UK who have always been supportive and available to help.

Thanks for the amazing photography by Steve Painter and the food styling by Lucy McKelvie who have brought my recipes to life. I know Steve also wants to thank Sonny Elliott of Rock-a-nore Fisheries in Hastings (rockanore.co.uk, +44 (0)1424 445 425) who kindly demonstrated preparing fish for the step-by-step photography and allowed us to shoot their curing and smoking process (page 50).